CITIZENS' RIGHTS

A Guide to Public Records and Open Meetings Laws

David H. Eckenrode
with
The North Carolina Attorney General's Office

Library of Congress Control Number: 2003096650

Copywrite © 2003

All rights reserved. No part of this publication may be reproduced or transmitted in any form or by any means, electronic or mechanical, including photocopy, recording, or any information retrieval system.

Research Competed July 2002

ISBN 0-9774534-0-5

Free copies are available to the public while supply (2nd Printing) lasts.
Second Printing, Ed 2

Professional Support and Technical Services, LLC

For
Victoria Rose, future Pulitzer Prize winner
and
Jason, Senator, State of California

PREFACE

This manual is intended as a guide to two extremely important bodies of North Carolina law - the public records law and the open meetings law. These laws require that government agencies in North Carolina allow citizens to examine their records and attend their official meetings. Although these are simple requirements, they embody one of our most fundamental principles - that government "of the people" only works when the people know what the government is doing. That is why open government, is so crucial to the survival and health of the State.

This manual explains the kinds of records and meetings that are open to public access. It also explains those circumstances in which government agencies, in order to best serve the public or protect citizens' privacy, are permitted to keep some information confidential.

David H. Eckenrode
December 2002

Contents

Introduction 1

Part I The Public Records Law and the Open Meetings Law 6

   The Public Records Law 6

      The Right to Inspect and Get Copies of Public Records 6

      Public Records Defined 6

      Materials Considered to be Public Records 8

      Government Agencies must Permit Inspection and Furnish Copies of Records 10

      Inspect or Get Copies of Public Records 11

      Procedure for Requesting to Inspect Records 11

      Getting or Making Copies of Public Records 12

      Fees for Public Records 14

      Agencies are Only Required to Permit Inspection or Provide Copies of Written or Recorded Information 15

      Inspecting or Getting Copies of Records that Contain Both Public and Confidential Information 16

      Civil Actions Requiring Agencies to Disclose Public Records 17

      Certain Government Records are Exempt from Disclosure 19

   The Open Meetings Law 20

      Meetings of Public Bodies to be Conducted Openly 20

      Official Meetings of Public Bodies are Open to the Public 20

      Public Bodies Defined 20

      Official Meetings Defined 21

      Public Notice of Official Meetings 21

      Open Meetings Law Only Guarantees the Public's Right to Attend Official Meetings 23

      Public's Right to Listen to Electronic Meetings 24

      Public's Right to Record Official Meeting 24

      Regulation of Broadcasting and Recording at Official Meetings 24

Public Bodies May Not Conceal the Subject of their Actions or Deliberations 25

Public Bodies May Not Vote by Secret Ballot 25

Emergency Meetings of Public Bodies 25

Public Bodies Must Keep Minutes of Official Meetings 26

Closed Sessions of Official Meetings.. 26

Procedure for Holding a Closed Session 27

Permitted Purposes for Holding Closed Sessions 27

Subjects No Longer Permitted in Closed Sessions................................ 30

Civil Actions for Violations of Open Meetings Law................................. 30

Certain Groups Are Subject/Not Subject to the Open Meetings Law....... 34

Part II Exceptions, Modifications, and References to Public Records and Open Meetings in the North Carolina General Statutes............... 35

Courts Shall Be Open.. 35

Discovery in Civil Actions - Protective Orders....................................... 36

Medical Records Subpoenaed in Civil Actions 36

Removal of District Attorneys 36

Clerks of Superior Court - Court Records... 36

Gag Orders - Courts May Not Issue Gag Orders on Public Records...... 37

Investigations of Child Abuse, Neglect or Dependency 37

Central Registry of Child Abuse, Neglect and Dependency Cases 37

Juveniles 38

    Probable Cause Hearings for Juveniles 14 and Older 38

    Adjudicatory Hearings for Juveniles.. 38

    Dispositional Hearings for Juveniles... 38

    Juvenile Delinquency Records in the Hands of Division of Youth Services 38

    Review Hearings for Juvenile Placements After Termination of Parental Rights 38

    Confidentiality of Juvenile Records... 39

    Expunction of Records of Delinquent and Undisciplined Juveniles.......... 39

    Expunction of Juvenile Criminal Convictions 40

Employment Discrimination Charges Investigated by Office of Administrative Hearings 40
Privledged Communications 40
    Communications Between Physician and Patient 40
    Physician-Patient Privilege Waived in Child Abuse Cases 41
    Communications Between Clergy and Communicants 41
    Communications Between Psychologist and Client or Patient 41
    School Counselor Privilege 41
    Communications Between Marital and Family Therapist and Client 41
    Marital Counseling Information in Alimony and Divorce Actions 41
    Social Worker Privilege 42
    Counselor Privilege 42
    Husband and Wife as Witness in Civil Actions 42
    Husband and Wife as Witness in Criminal Action 42
Records of Hearings into Past Sexual Behavior of Rape Victims 42
Jury Lists 42
Abortion Data Collected by Department of Human Resources 43
Probation Officers' Records; Parole Records 43
Expunction of Criminal Charges 44
DNA Database 44
Grand Jury Proceedings 44
Discovery in Criminal Cases 44
Crime Victim Compensation - Reports 45
Social Security Numbers Used for Drivers License Administration 46
Division of Motor Vehicles 47
Motor Vehicle Collision Reports 48
Pre-Adoption Reports 49
Adoption Records 50
Child Custody and Visitation Mediation 50
Banking and Financial 50
Insurance 54

Utilities	61
Proposed Changes for Bus Company Rates	62
Customer Information Submitted to 911 Emergency Telephone Systems	62
Lists of Partners in Professional Partnerships	63
Mine Accident Reports	63
Securities Dealers and Salesmen Registration	64
Investment Advisors	65
Athlete Agents	65
Trademark Registration	66
Licensed Professionals and Professional Boards	66
Attorney Licensing Records	66
North Carolina State Bar	66
Record of Registered Barbers and Apprentices	66
Roster of Licensed Contractors	66
Records of Plumbing, Heating, and Fire Sprinkler Contractors Board	66
Registry of Licensed Electrical Contractors	67
Cosmetologist Records	67
Board Investigations of Engineers and Surveyors	67
Landscape Contractor Register	67
Geologist Licensing Records	67
Reports to Board of Medical Examiners Concerning Physician Privileges and Malpractice Insurance	68
Physician Licensing and Disciplinary Records	68
Elections of Board of Dental Examiners	69
Dentist Licensing and Disciplinary Records	69
Chiropractor Access to Laboratory Records	69
Meetings of North Carolina Medical Veterinary Board	70
Board of Podiatry Examiners - List of Licensed Podiatrists	70
North Carolina Board of Opticians	70
Psychologist Licensing and Disciplinary Records	70
Fee-Based Practicing Pastoral Counselors	70

    State Board of Sanitarian Examiners 71
    North Carolina Real Estate Commission... 71
    Occupational Licensing Board Annual Reports....................................... 71
    Occupational Licensing Boards 71
    North Carolina Hearing Aid Dealers and Fitters Board 72
    North Carolina Appraisal Board 72
Pharmacy Records.. 72
Expunction of Records Under the North Carolina Controlled Substances Act.... 72
Controlled Substance Records 73
Records of Treatment for Drug Dependence.. 73
Department of Labor Investigation Records 73
Private Personnel Service Advisory Council.. 73
Elevator Safety Act, Amusement Device Safety Act, and Occupational Safety
    and Health Act Records.. 73
State Advisory Council on Occupational Safety and Health 74
Toxic Vapors Act - Conditional Discharge 74
Safety and Health Review Board... 74
Occupational Safety and Health Programs of State and Local Agencies 74
Hazardous Chemical Emergency Information to be Supplied to Fire Chiefs 74
Hazardous Chemical Emergency Information to be Supplied to Health Care
    Providers... 75
Community Information on Hazardous Chemicals.. 75
Employment Security Commission 76
North Carolina Industrial Commission 77
Southeast Interstate Low-Level Radioactive Waste Management Commission. 78
Revenue Statistics... 78
Proposed Property Tax Appraisal Schedules, Standards and Rules.................. 79
Taxpayer Information Held by State Agencies for Debt Collection 79
Agriculture Statistics.. 79
Poultry Products Inspection Act Information... 80
Commercial Fertilizer Grade-Tonnage Reports... 80

Permission to Release Genetically Engineered Organisms 80
Assessment on Hog Purchases.. 81
Receipt of Public Assistance 81
Day Care Inspection Plans 82
Child Support - Location of Absent Parents... 82
Marine Fisheries Commission Records 83
Coastal Land-Use Plans.. 83
Areas of Environmental Concern... 84
Forest Product Assessments.. 84
Division of Criminal Information 84
Criminal Record Checks of School Employees 84
Criminal Record Checks of Employees of Hospitals, Nursing Homes, Mental Health Authorities, and Mental Health Contract Agencies 84
Elementary and Secondary Education 85
    Public Records.. 85
    Open Meetings 85
    Proceedings of State Board of Education 85
    Uniform Education Reporting System... 85
    Census of Children with Special Needs.. 86
    Records Relating to Children with Special Needs................................. 86
    Classification of Children with Special Needs....................................... 86
    Statewide Student Testing Program Scores 87
    Outcome-Based Education Program 87
    Minutes of Local Boards of Education 87
    Public School Teacher Complaint/Commendation Files 87
    Public School Student Records 87
Community College Records and Meetings 87
University of North Carolina Health-Care Liability Insurance Records............. 88
List of Escheated and Abandoned Property 88
Certification of Holdings of Unclaimed and Abandoned Property 88
Legislator Access to State Agency Information 89

Lobbyist Expense Reports 89
Disclosure of Confidential Information by Legislators Forbidden 89
General Assembly Candidates' Statements of Economic Interest 89
Legislative Ethics Committee 89
Communications Between Legislators and Legislative Employees 90
Inspection of Archived Public Records 91
Confidential Information Relating to Clients at Facilities for People with Mental Illnesses, Developmental Disabilities, and Substance Abuse Problems .. 91
State Libraries and State Publications 94
Library User Records 94
Personnel Records of Government Employees 95
National Guard Records 99
Medical Records in the Public Health System 100
Birth Certificates 100
Communicable Diseases 100
Solid Waste Management 101
State Center for Health Statistics 101
Autopsies 101
Domiciliary Homes for People Who are Aged or Disabled 102
Hospital Inspections 103
Hospital Medical Review Committees 103
Patient Information at Health Care Facilities 103
Peer Review Committees for Nursing Homes 105
Nursing Home Complaint Investigations 105
North Carolina Medical Database Commission 106
Attorney-Client Communications 106
Confidentiality of Tax Information 108
Trade Secrets 109
Settlement Records 110
Criminal Investigations and Criminal Intelligence Information 110
Business or Industrial Projects 113

Public Contract Bidding 114
Teachers' and State Employees' Comprehensive Major Medical Plan 115
Highway Construction Bids 115
Highway Construction - Construction Diaries and Bid Analyses 115
Test Drilling or Boring 115
Organizations Receiving State Funds 115
Joint Meetings of Legislative Budget Committees 116
Bids for State Government Supplies, Materials, Contractual Services and Equipment 116
Local Government Small Contracts 116
Construction and Repair Work Done by State or Local Employees 116
Sewage Pretreatment Program Applications 117
Environmental Management Commission Investigation Records 117
Water and Air Pollution Reports 117
Public Hospital Boards 118
Government Bodies Not Subject to the Open Meetings Law 118
Legislative Commissions, Committees and Standing Subcommittees 120
Repayment of Money Owed by Employees and Officials of the State and of Boards of Education and Boards of Community Colleges 121
North Carolina Child Fatality Prevention System 121
State Health Plan Purchasing Alliances 121
North Carolina Partnership for Children, Inc 122
Deliberations of the Environmental Management Commission 122
Minutes of Board of Transportation Meetings 123
Governor's Advocacy Council for Persons with Disabilities 123
Economic Development Board Annual Reports 123
Meetings of North Carolina Mutual Burial Association Commission 123
North Carolina Center for Missing Persons 123
State Auditor Work Papers 124
Contested Case Administrative Hearings 124
Township Boundaries 125

Regular and Special Meetings of Boards of County Commissioners................ 125
Minutes of Proceedings of County Boards of Commissioners and Municipal Councils 126
County and Municipal Ordinance Books.. 126
Public Hearings Before County Boards of Commissioners and City Councils .. 126
County and Municipal Managers' Annual Reports.. 127
Jail Inspections 127
County, Municipal, and Urban Service Districts.. 128
Regional Planning Commissions 128
Local Government Budgets 128
Joint Municipal Electric Agencies 129
Municipal Annexation 129
Regular and Special Meetings of City and Town Councils 129
City and Town Council Minutes 130
Local Preservation Commission Meetings.. 130
Meetings and Annual Reports of Regional Councils of Government................ 130
Meetings of Regional Sports Authorities... 131
Redevelopment Commissions 131
Metropolitan Water District Financial Reports... 131
Extension of Water and Sewer Districts 131
Voter Registration Records 131
Ballot Counting 132
Registers of Absentee Ballots... 133
State Board of Elections 133
Voter Registration for Municipal Annexations and Incorporations 134
Division of Veteran Affairs 134
Public Policy Exceptions to Public Records Law Disclosure Requirements 134

Part III Exemptions from the Public Records Law and the Open Meetings Law for Certain Counties and Municipalities........................ 137
Admissions Fee Tax Returns.. 137
Board of Education Discussions of Voting Rights Litigation 137

    Discrimination Investigations and Proceedings 137
    Food and Beverage Tax Returns... 138
    Official City Map Open for Inspection 138
    Room Occupancy and Tourism Development Tax Returns............................. 138
        Counties.. 138
        Municipalities and Townships 140

Part IV Table of Cases 143

Part V North Carolina Attorney General Opinions........................151

Part VI Some Common Public Records and Where They Can Be Found 157

Part VII State Government Offices..161
    Principal State Departments 161
    State Licensing Agencies 167

Index 171

Introduction

In North Carolina, two bodies of law guarantee public access to government records and meetings. These two bodies are known as the public records law and the open meetings law.[1] The public records law was first adopted in 1935, and it has been amended several times since then. The open meetings law was adopted in 1971. It has also been amended.

Part I of this manual explains the public records and open meetings laws. For the public records law, Part I describes the kinds of records that the public may inspect. It also describes the kinds of State and local government agencies that must disclose their records. Part I tells how citizens may enforce the public records law if government agencies do not allow records to be examined.

For the open meetings law, Part I describes which State and local public bodies must allow the public to attend their meetings. It explains the kind of notice public bodies must give the public before holding meetings. The open meetings law allows public bodies to hold "closed sessions" and exclude the public when it discusses certain subjects. Part I describes when and how public bodies may do this. Finally, Part I tells how people may enforce the open meetings law if public bodies hold private meetings or don't give proper notice of their meetings.

There are many exceptions to the public records and open meetings laws. In some cases, government agencies are allowed to keep records confidential or keep the public from attending their meetings. In other cases, access to government records or meetings is limited. In still other cases, government agencies are prohibited from disclosing records or allowing the public at their meetings.

Finding all of these exceptions in the North Carolina General Statutes is difficult. Some of them are listed in the public records and open meetings laws, themselves. However, many more exceptions are scattered throughout other sections of the General Statutes. The General Statutes do not contain any index or other reference to all these exceptions. All the known exceptions, including the ones found in the public records

---

The "Freedom of Information Act" is a federal law that permits access to records of federal government agencies. It does not apply to records of State and local agencies in North Carolina.

law, the open meetings law, and in other parts of the General Statutes, are collected and summarized in Part II of this manual. For the most part, the exceptions are listed in the order they appear in the General Statutes. In some cases, exceptions dealing with certain subjects are grouped together for easy reference.[2]

Readers who want to find exceptions by subject or agency should refer to the alphabetical Index at the end of the manual.

Readers should notice that there are different types of public records exceptions. If a record is "not a public record," this simply means that the agency with the record is not required to disclose it to the public. In this situation the agency still has the option of disclosing it, and they may do so at their discretion. On the other hand, many statutes say that a certain record is "confidential" and the agency "may not disclose" it to the public. In this situation, the agency has no discretion and it may not disclose the record at all.

Many sections of the North Carolina General Statutes simply confirm that certain agencies, records and meetings are subject to the public records and open meetings laws. These statutory sections confirming public access to records and meetings are also listed and summarized in Part II. As with the exceptions, they are listed in the order they appear in the General Statutes. The Index will help those who want to find any of these references by subject or agency.[3]

The public records and open meetings laws apply to local governments in North Carolina. However, the North Carolina General Assembly has allowed some counties, cities and towns to pass ordinances that exempt certain documents and meetings from these laws. Part III of the manual describes the records and meetings that local governments have been permitted to exempt, and it lists the counties, cities and towns that have been given these exemptions.

For example, personnel records of government employees are generally exempt from public disclosure. However, there are nine separate sections of the General Statutes describing these personnel record exceptions. For the convenience of readers, all nine sections are discussed together in the section called Personnel Records of Government Employees.

A note on how to interpret these sections that confirm the openness of records and meetings. The fact that certain records and meetings are referenced in the General Statutes as being accessible or open to the public does not mean that all other records and meetings are confidential or closed. Unless there is a law specifically exempting a record or a meeting from these laws, it should be assumed that the public has access to that record or meeting.

As one might expect, some disagreements over public records and open meetings have ended up in the courts. Some of the written court decisions in these cases give guidance to agencies and the public in resolving future disputes over public records and meetings.

Court decisions on public records and open meetings are referred to throughout this manual. Discussions of these decisions are found directly in the sections of the manual dealing with the subjects that were at issue in the cases. A list of all the cases cited in the manual is found in Part IV. This list includes a brief summary of each case and the pages of the manual on which each case is mentioned or discussed.

One of the duties of the Attorney General is to give formal opinions to government agencies. These opinions often help government agencies, the public and the courts resolve legal disagreements. Since the public records law was first adopted in 1935, North Carolina's Attorneys General have issued several opinions on the public records and open meetings laws. This manual notes many of these Attorney General opinions on public records and open meetings.[4] These opinions are mentioned directly in the sections of the manual dealing with the subjects they address. A list of all the opinions cited in the manual is found in Part V. This list includes a brief summary of each opinion and the pages of the manual on which the opinion is mentioned and discussed. A note of caution for the layperson. Opinions issued by the Attorney General's Office are not law; they are mere opinion. The Office of Attorney General is a political office and opinions issued by that office may reflect a political flavor.

Part VI of the manual lists some of the North Carolina State and local government offices that keep public records frequently sought by the public. For each of these offices, there is a list of the kinds of documents that can be found there. Part V is arranged by office, not by type of record. Under each office the records that can be found there are listed alphabetically.

Finally, Part VII of the manual lists the names, addresses, and phone numbers of North Carolina's principal State departments, agencies and licensing boards. It also contains the addresses and phone numbers for all the clerk of court and register of deeds offices in North Carolina.

There are many public records and open meetings issues that are not addressed in the North Carolina General Statutes and not resolved by court decisions. This

---

Some Attorney General opinions on public records and open meetings are now obsolete, either because the statutes have been repealed or amended, or because court decisions have given different interpretations. The opinions that no longer apply are not included in this manual.

manual attempts to discuss only those issues that are addressed by statutes, court decisions, or Attorney General opinions. I've tried not to fill in the gaps in the law or interpret the law where there is not any North Carolina legal authority on the subject. Where the manual includes our interpretations it is usually because they are so widely accepted by the legal community that they are undisputed. In the few places where this manual makes these kinds of interpretations, they usually include a statement such as "it is usually assumed that . . ."[5]

North Carolina does not have one comprehensive law dealing with the privacy of citizens' records. Privacy laws are scattered throughout the North Carolina General Statutes. This manual includes statutes that restrict the public from examining government records on other people or businesses. (Most of these statutes are discussed in Part II, since they involve exceptions to the public records law).

Some statutes prohibit government agencies from inspecting private individuals' or businesses' records. Other statutes restrict government agencies from sharing the records of individuals or businesses with other agencies. Some of these statutes are mentioned in this manual. However, since the focus of this manual is public access to government records, this manual does not contain all of the statutes in these two categories.

Another subject not addressed directly in the manual is public hearings. A public hearing is a type of government meeting where the public usually has the right to speak or give input into government decisions. Not all meetings of public bodies are public hearings. At most meetings of public bodies (other than public hearings) the public has a right to attend and listen, but they don't necessarily have the right to participate in the meeting. The open meetings law only deals with access to meetings. Since the focus of this manual is on the open meetings law and access to meetings, the manual makes only occasional references to public hearings. However, the manual does discuss government hearings that are not open to the general public, or that are limited to certain people.

Some sections of the public records law regulate the preservation of government records. Rules of the Department of Cultural Resources say when government agencies must keep records, when they may destroy old records, and when they must

---

Two booklets by David Lawrence of the Institute of Government at the University of North Carolina at Chapel Hill provide broader interpretations of the public records and open meetings laws, based on extensive research on other states' statutes and court decisions. David M. Lawrence, *Interpreting North Carolina's Public Records Law* (Institute of Government, 1987) and David M. Lawrence, *Open Meetings and Local Governments in North Carolina*, (Institute of Government, Third Edition, Revised 1991).

transfer records to the Department for archiving. Since this manual focuses on public access to government records, the sections on preservation of records are not discussed here. For more information on preservation and destruction of records, readers may look at Sections 132-3 through 132-5.1 and sections 132-7 through 132-8.2 of the public records law. They may also contact the Department of Cultural Resources.

Part I
The Public Records Law and the Open Meetings Law

General

Part I of the Citizen's Rights Manual describes the basic provisions of the public records and open meetings laws. Court decisions and Attorney General opinions are noted as relevant provisions are discussed.

There are many exceptions to the public records and open meetings laws. Some of these are found directly in the laws themselves. Many other exceptions are found in other parts of the North Carolina General Statutes. These exceptions are discussed in Part II of this manual.

The Public Records Law

Public Policy - Public Records and Information are the Property of the People - N.C. Gen. Stat. § 132-1(b)

The North Carolina General Assembly has declared as a matter of public policy that the public records and public information compiled by the agencies of North Carolina government or its subdivisions are the property of the people.

The Right to Inspect and Get Copies of Public Records - N.C. Gen. Stat. § 132-6

Any person has the right to inspect, examine, and get copies of public records.

Public Records Defined - N.C. Gen. Stat. § 132-1(a)

Public records are documentary materials that are either made or received by government agencies in North Carolina in carrying on public business. Public records include materials written or created by the government and its employees. They also include materials written or made by private people or companies and submitted to the government, regardless of whether those materials were required or requested by the government, or whether they were sent to the government voluntarily at the private person's initiative.

Public records include documentary materials that government agencies are required by law to make or collect. (N.C. Gen. Stat. § 132-1) Public records also include materials that government agencies make or collect at their discretion in carrying on government business. *News & Observer Pub. Co. v. Wake County Hospital System, Inc.*, 55 N.C. App. 1, 284 S.E.2d 542 (1981),*cert. denied*, 305 N.C. 302, 291 S.E.2d 151 (1982).

The decision in *Wake County Hospital System* confirmed a 1971 opinion, in which the North Carolina Attorney General said that public records included not only documents required to be made or received by law, but also included any other documents made by government officials in their public employment capacity. 41 N.C.A.G. 199 (1971).

In *Durham Herald Co. v. North Carolina Low-Level Radioactive Waste Management Authority*, 110 N.C. App. 607, 430 S.E.2d 441 (1993), a newspaper sought to inspect documents produced by private companies who were under contract with the Authority (a state agency) to study the siting, operating and closing of waste facilities. At the time the newspaper sought inspection of these documents, the companies had not yet turned the documents over to the Authority.

The North Carolina Court of Appeals ruled that the documents were not yet public records subject to required disclosure. The Court noted that under the Authority's operating statute, the Authority "shall receive" contractors' documents "as the Authority deems appropriate," and all these documents "shall become the property of the State." N.C. Gen. Stat. § 104G-6(a)(18). Reading this provision together with the public records law section defining public records as documents "received" by government agencies in the course of public business (N.C. Gen. Stat. § 132-1), the Court concluded that the contractor documents in this case did not become the property of the State until after the documents were received by the Authority. Since the documents were not yet the property of the State, they were not subject to disclosure as public records.

Similarly, in a 1975 opinion the North Carolina Attorney General said that documents being worked on for a county by a private contractor were not public records. A county contracted with a private company to conduct a property revaluation for ad valorem taxes. The company's employees recorded data on appraisal cards. This information had not yet been turned over to the county. The Attorney General said that the appraisal cards were not subject to public inspection yet because they had not been made by the county, and had not yet been received by the county. 45 N.C.A.G. 55 (1975). However, in a 1962 opinion the Attorney General said that completed tax listing abstracts are public records subject to public inspection. 37 N.C.A.G. 85 (1962).

In *Advance Publications, Inc. v. Elizabeth City*, 53 N.C. App. 504, 281 S.E.2d 69 (1981), a city retained an engineer as a consultant to inspect its water treatment plant. Although the engineer was not a city employee, the North Carolina Court of Appeals ruled that a letter he wrote to the city manager was a public record subject to disclosure. The court held that the letter was received by the city in connection with public business, and it was therefore a public record.

Materials Considered to be Public Records - N.C. Gen. Stat. § 132-1

Public records include documents, papers, letters, maps, books, photographs, films, sound recordings, magnetic or other tapes, electronic data-processing records, artifacts, or other documentary material, regardless of physical form or characteristics.

In a 1973 opinion the North Carolina Attorney General said that municipal books and papers, such as budgets, bank statements, tax levies, utility accounts and minutes of meetings are all public records which may be inspected by members of the public. 43 N.C.A.G. 274 (1973).

In *News & Observer Pub. Co. v. Poole*, 330 N.C. 465, 412 S.E.2d 7 (1992), the North Carolina Supreme Court refused to infer that there is a deliberative process privilege which exempts preliminary drafts of government reports from disclosure under the public records law. In *Poole*, two members of an investigatory government commission wrote drafts of a final report for the commission. A newspaper sought to inspect those drafts. The Court ruled that those drafts were public records.

In *North Carolina Press Asso. v. Spangler*, 87 N.C. App. 169, 360 S.E.2d 138 (1987), the North Carolina Court of Appeals also found that a public university was not justified in refusing to release reports to a newspaper based on the fact that they were preliminary, intergovernmental communications.

In *S.E.T.A. UNC-CH, Inc. v. Huffines*, 101 N.C. App. 292, 399 S.E.2d 340 (1991), an animal rights group sought disclosure of applications for approval to do proposed experimental research on animals at a State university. The university refused to disclose the applications, basing its refusal in part on a public policy argument that disclosure might subject researchers to violence and harassment that would have a chilling effect on university research.

The North Carolina Court of Appeals rejected the argument that all of the information in the application could be withheld for this reason. The Court held that information describing the proposed experiments should be disclosed as public records.

However, the Court also found that there was a public policy privacy interest for researchers and their staffs. The court held that the names, telephone numbers, addresses, department names, and departmental experience of researchers and their staffs need not be disclosed. Without explanation, the court also ruled that disapproved applications need not be disclosed.

Electronic Data-Processing Records - N.C. Gen. Stat. § 132-6.1

In 1995, the North Carolina General Assembly added some provisions to the public records law to ease public access to public records stored in government computers.

After June 30, 1996, no public agency may acquire a new electronic data-processing system for the storage, manipulation or retrieval of public records unless it first determines that the system will not hinder the agency's ability to permit inspection or make copies of public records.

Every public agency is required to create an index of its computer databases. The index must include at least:

1) a list of the data fields;

2) a description of the format or record layout;

3) information on how often the database is updated;

4) a list of any data fields to which public access is restricted;

5) a description of each form in which the database can be copied or reproduced using the agency's computer facilities; and

6) a schedule of fees for the production of copies in each available form.

These indexes of computer databases must be created on the following schedule:

1) State agencies by July 1, 1996;

2) Municipalities with populations of 10,000 or more, counties with populations of 25,000 or more, and public hospitals in those counties, by July 1, 1997;

3) Municipalities with populations of less than 10,000, counties with populations of less than 25,000, and public hospitals in those counties by July 1, 1998; and

4) Other political subdivisions and their agencies by June 30, 1998.

Electronic databases created before these deadlines may be indexed at the option of these agencies.

The indexes of computer databases, themselves, are public records.

These provisions do not require public agencies to:

1) retain obsolete hardware of software;
2) create a computer database that it has not created; or
3) disclose its software security, including passwords.

Government Agencies must Permit Inspection and Furnish Copies of Records - N.C. Gen. Stat. § 132-1(a)

Agencies of North Carolina government and its subdivisions must permit inspection and furnish copies of public records. These agencies include all public offices, officers and officials (elected or appointed), staffers, institutions, boards, commissions, bureaus, councils, departments, authorities and other units of government. State, county, city and town governments and their departments, officials and employees are included,[6] as are all other political subdivisions and special districts.

United States federal government agencies are not covered by the North Carolina public records law. Federal agencies are subject to the federal Freedom of Information Act.

In *News & Observer Co. v. Wake County Hospital System, Inc.*, 55 N.C. App. 1, 284 S.E.2d 542, the North Carolina Court of Appeals held that a hospital system organized as a nonprofit corporation was a county agency whose records were subject to the public records law. The court found that although the corporation exercised some authority independently from the county, the county supervised and controlled the corporation to the extent that the corporation should be considered an agency of the county. Among the factors considered by the court in reaching this conclusion were: (1) the corporation's assets would transfer to the county upon dissolution; (2) county commissioners approved all vacancies on the corporation's board; (3) the corporation leased its premises from the county for $1.00 a year; (4) the county commissioners reviewed and approved the corporation's annual budget; (5) the county conducted supervisory audits of the corporation's books; (6) the corporation reported it charges and rates to the county; (7) the corporation was financed by county bond orders; (8) revenue collected from the bond orders was revenue of the county; (9) and the corporation could not change its corporate existence or amend its articles of incorporation without the county's written consent.

In a 1973 opinion the North Carolina Attorney General said that municipal books and papers, such as budgets, bank statements, tax levies, utility accounts and minutes of meetings are all public records which may be inspected by members of the public. 43 N.C.A.G. 274 (1973).

Inspect or Get Copies of Public Records - N.C. Gen. Stat. § 132-6

Any person may inspect and get copies of public records. Government agencies may not require people to disclose their purpose or motive for inspecting or getting copies of public records. It is generally accepted that a government agency may not refuse to allow a person to inspect or get copies of public records because of who the person is, or why the person wants the records. In a 1969 opinion, the North Carolina Attorney General said that access to public records should be permitted regardless of the announced or unannounced purposes for which information acquired from the records will be used. 40 N.C.A.G. 709, 710 (1969). In a 1973 opinion, the Attorney General said any person may demand inspection of public records even if his motives are based on mere speculation or idle curiosity. 42 N.C.A.G. 229 (1973).

Corporations are considered to be "persons" who may inspect and examine public records. *Advance Publications, Inc. v. Elizabeth City*, 53 N.C. App. 504, 281 S.E.2d 69 (1981).

Procedure for Requesting to Inspect Records

The public records law does not describe any specific procedure that a person must follow in requesting to inspect[7] public records. There is no specific form for making requests. There is no requirement that requests be in writing. There is no requirement that the person making the request refer specifically to the public records law when making the request.

The law also does not require that requests to inspect public records be made a certain time in advance, and the law does not have any specific waiting period between the time of the request and the time of inspection.

The public records law says that inspection and examination of records should be allowed at "reasonable times" and under the supervision of the agency. N.C. Gen. Stat. § 132-6. This means that agencies may, within reason, determine how and when they will allow inspection of records. Agencies may require that an employee watch and supervise a person who is inspecting the records, and agencies may take other precautionary measures to ensure that inspected records are not damaged or taken. Agencies also may make reasonable restrictions on inspections to preserve public records that are old or in poor condition. N.C. Gen. Stat. § 132-6(f). Agencies may take a reasonable amount of time to collect and present records for inspection. Agencies

---

This section deals only with inspection of records. Requests for copies of records are discussed below.

may not, however, withhold records based on the agency's belief that immediate release of the records would not be "prudent or timely." *North Carolina Press Asso. v. Spangler*, 87 N.C. App. 169, 360 S.E.2d 138 (1987).

Normally, a request to any employee in a government office is sufficient to get access to records in that office. Technically, however, it is the "custodian" of public records who is required to allow those records to be inspected. The public official in charge of a government office is the custodian of the public records in that office. N.C. Gen. Stat. § 132-2.

Government agencies that are holding public records of other agencies just for storage or safekeeping, or just to provide data processing, are not "custodians" of those records. N.C. Gen. Stat. § 132-6(a). This means that these holding agencies are not required to allow inspection of those records.

Getting or Making Copies of Public Records

The public records law says that anyone may obtain copies of public records. N.C. Gen. Stat. § 132-1(b).

There are several ways in which people might get copies. They might simply ask the agency to make copies for them. Some people make their own copies by using agency copy machines or printers. Some people bring their own copying equipment to the agency and use that equipment to make copies. Some people might request to take public records to another location (such as a library, copy store, or their own office) to make copies using other equipment.

The public records law does not specify how copies may be obtained, and it does not mention any of these methods, specifically. Since copying of public records is subject to agency supervision,[8] agencies may have different rules about members of the public using agency equipment, making their own copies, or removing documents to make copies elsewhere.

However, the public records law makes it clear that agencies must "furnish" copies of public records to people who request them. N.C. Gen. Stat. § 132-6(a). At the least, this means that agencies must make copies of public records for people who request them. Also, in a 1973 opinion the North Carolina Attorney General said that a person who wants copies of public records may make copies using his own clerical

---

For example, agencies may make reasonable restrictions on the copying of records if necessary to preserve records that are old or in poor condition. N.C. Gen. Stat. § 132-6(f).

assistants. 42 N.C.A.G. 229 (1973).

There is no specific procedure for requesting copies of public records. There is no specific form for making requests. For most public records, there is no requirement that requests be in writing.[9] There is no requirement that the person making the request refer specifically to the public records law when making the request.

The law also does not require that requests for copies be made a certain time in advance. Agencies are required to furnish copies "as promptly as possible." N.C. Gen. Stat. § 132-6(a). However, agencies are not required to provide copies outside of their usual business hours. N.C. Gen. Stat. § 132-6.2(d).

Normally, a request to any employee in a government office is sufficient to get copies of records in that office. Technically, however, it is the "custodian" of public records who is required to furnish copies. The public official in charge of a government office is the custodian of the public records in that office. N.C. Gen. Stat. § 132-2.

Government agencies that are holding public records of other agencies just for storage or safekeeping, or just to provide data processing, are not "custodians" of those records. N.C. Gen. Stat. § 132-6(a). This means that these holding agencies are not required to furnish copies of those records.

If an agency has the capability to provide copies of public records in different kinds of media (for example, in print or on computer disc), people requesting copies may choose to get copies in any and all the media available. The agency may not refuse to provide copies in a particular medium because it has made, or prefers to make, copies available in another medium. However, agencies may assess different copying fees for different media as prescribed by law. N.C. Gen. Stat. § 132-6.2(a). Agencies are not required to put a record into electronic medium if that record is not kept in electronic medium.

People requesting copies of public records may ask for certified or uncertified copies. N.C. Gen. Stat. § 132-6.2(b). Certified copies are ones that include a statement by the agency that the copy is a true and accurate copy of the original.

People requesting copies of computer databases may be required to make their requests in writing. Agencies must respond as promptly as possible. If the request is granted, copies must be provided as soon as reasonably possible. If the request is denied, the agency must explain the reason at the time of denial. If asked to do so, the agency must promptly put in writing the reason for denial. N.C. Gen. Stat. § 132-6.2(c).

However, people who are requesting copies of computer databases may be required to make their requests in writing. N.C. Gen. Stat. § 132-6.2(c)

Fees for Public Records

Government agencies may not charge fees for inspecting public records.[10] Under certain circumstances fees may be charged for copies of public records.

In general, the public records law says that copies of public records may be obtained free or at minimal cost, unless there is another law that specifies otherwise.[11] "Minimal cost" means the actual cost of reproducing the record. N.C. Gen. Stat. § 132-1(b).

Fees for certifying copies of public records are to be charged as prescribed by law. N.C. Gen. Stat. § 132-6.2(b).

For uncertified copies of public records, agencies may not charge fees that are more than the actual cost to the agency of making the copy. "Actual cost" is defined as "direct, chargeable costs related to the reproduction of a public record as determined by generally accepted accounting principles." N.C. Gen. Stat. § 132-6.2(b).

The law does not give examples of actual costs. Presumably, they include the cost of the paper or computer disc on which a copy might be provided. The law does not say whether actual costs also include the cost of the use or depreciation of copy machines. The law says that actual cost may not include costs the agency would have incurred if the copy request had not been made. N.C. Gen. Stat. § 132-6.2(b). For example, if an agency already has a copy machine for its own internal use, it may not charge as part of its public records copying fee a fraction of the purchase cost of the copy machine.

Under most circumstances, the fees agencies charge for uncertified copies of public records also may not include the labor costs of agency employees who make the copies. However, if making the copies involves extensive clerical or supervisory assistance by agency employees, the agency may charge a special service charge (in

---

However, for a limited period of time after October 1, 1995, agencies responding to requests for inspection of documents may recover a service charge for the cost of separating confidential information from otherwise public records. For details, see *Inspecting and Getting Copies of Records that Contain Both Public and Confidential Information*, below.

Several government agencies that provide large volumes of public records to the public have specific statutory fees or statutory permission to establish their own fees for providing copies of the records. For example, clerks of court (N.C. Gen. Stat. § 7A-308), registers of deeds (N.C. Gen. Stat. § 161-10), and the Division of Motor Vehicles (N.C. Gen. Stat. § 20-26) all have their own statutory fee schedules for providing copies of public records.

addition to actual duplication costs). This service charge must be reasonable and must be based on actual labor costs. N.C. Gen. Stat. § 132-6.2(b).

For a limited time after October 1, 1995, agencies may also charge a service charge for the labor involved in separating confidential information from public records before providing requested copies of those records, if that is necessary. N.C. Gen. Stat. § 132-6(c). (This is discussed in more detail in *Inspecting and Getting Copies of Public Records that Contain Both Public and Confidential Information*, below).

Sometimes government agencies must make extensive use of information technology resources (for example, computer equipment and services) to respond to requests for copies of public records. This might happen if the request is particularly large. It might also happen if the request is for copies in a particular medium, and producing those copies involves an unusually extensive use of information technology resources. In these kinds of circumstances, agencies may charge a special service charge (in addition to actual duplication costs) to recover the cost involved in the extensive use of the information technology resources.

As prescribed by law, government agencies may charge different fees that represent the cost of providing copies of public records in different media. N.C. Gen. Stat. § 132-6.2(a). For example, there might be a different cost to the agency for providing a copy of a record on a computer disc, as opposed to a copy on paper. The agency may be permitted to charge a different fee to recover its different costs.

Agencies may charge fees to recover the costs of mailing copies of public records to people who request that copies be mailed to them. N.C. Gen. Stat. § 12-3.1(c).

Anyone who believes that he has been charged an unfair fee for copies of public records may ask the Information Resource Management Commission to mediate the dispute. N.C. Gen. Stat. § 132-6.2(b).

Agencies are Only Required to Permit Inspection or Provide Copies of Written or Recorded Information - N.C. Gen. Stat. § 132-6.2

The public records law requires that government agencies permit people to inspect or get copies of information that is in recorded form. The law does not indicate that government agencies are required to provide information verbally to people who request it.[12] The law also does not require that government agencies create or compile

---

By way of general policy, the public records law says that "public records and public information" of North Carolina government agencies "are the property of the people." N.C. Gen. Stat. § 132-1(b). However, there is nothing in the law stating that unrecorded information must be provided upon request to the public.

a record that does not exist. N.C. Gen. Stat. § 132-6.2(e).

An agency may agree voluntarily to compile or create a record upon request. If it does so, it may negotiate a reasonable service charge for creating or compiling the record.[13] N.C. Gen. Stat. § 132-6.2(e). Anyone who believes he has been charged an unfair fee for public information may ask the Information Resource Management Commission to mediate the dispute. N.C. Gen. Stat. § 132-6.2(b).

Inspecting or Getting Copies of Records that Contain Both Public and Confidential Information - N.C. Gen. Stat. §132-6(c)

Some records of public agencies are exempt from the public records law or are specifically designated as confidential by law. (These will be listed and discussed later in Part II).

Some records contain both public and confidential information. Government agencies may not refuse to permit inspection or to provide copies because public records contain some confidential information. Agencies must permit inspection and provide copies of the public parts of these records. They may do this by separating or redacting (making copies and crossing out) the confidential parts.

For a period of time after October 1, 1995, government agencies may collect a service charge for their costs in separating confidential information from public information. After a certain amount of time, however, agencies must bear the cost of separating confidential information. The dates after which agencies must bear the cost of separating confidential information are different for different types of government agencies. The schedule is as follows:

1) State agencies, after June 30, 1996;

2) Municipalities with populations of 10,000 or more, counties with populations of 25,000 or more, and public hospitals in those counties, after

---

Technically, the public records law only says that agencies are not required to create or compile records in response to requests for copies of records. N.C. Gen. Stat. § 132-6.2(e). The law does not say whether an agency must create or compile a record in response to requests to inspect records.

However, it is generally understood that agencies do not have to create or compile records in either situation. In a 1969 opinion the North Carolina Attorney General said that people who want information from the government are permitted to examine existing records. The public records law does not require government agencies to extract information from its existing records and rewrite it or compile it in another form for public *inspection.* (emphasis added) 40 N.C.A.G. 636 (1969)

June 30, 1997;

3) Municipalities with populations of less than 10,000, counties with populations of less than 25,000, and public hospitals in those counties, after June 30, 1998; and

4) Other political subdivisions and their agencies, after June 30, 1998.

Public Records Subject to Disclosure Do Not Become Confidential Simply Because They are Used By Another Agency in Confidential Proceedings

Government agencies often share public records with one another. Sometimes a government agency that gets records from another agency uses those records in a confidential proceeding. Do the records become confidential because the second agency is using them in a confidential proceeding?

Generally, no. For example, a police department conducting a criminal investigation may get drivers license records from the Division of Motor Vehicles for use in its investigation. Drivers license records are subject to public disclosure (N.C. Gen. Stat. § 20-27), but criminal investigation records of law enforcement agencies are not public records (N.C. Gen. Stat. § 132-1.4(a). The fact that the drivers license records are being used by police in a criminal investigation does not change their status as public records. They must still be disclosed if requested. N.C. Gen. Stat. § 132-1.4(f). However, the police do not have to reveal how the records might be relevant to the investigation.

In another example, a city council may use a closed session during one of its official meetings to discuss alleged misconduct by the director of a city agency. However, the misconduct might involve a contract entered into between the director's agency and a private company for services provided to the city. Although minutes of the council's discussion of the director's misconduct may be kept confidential (N.C. Gen. Stat. § 143-318.11(a)(6), the contract is a public record and must still be disclosed if requested. However, the council does not have to reveal how the contract might be relevant to the director's misconduct.

Civil Actions Requiring Agencies to Disclose Public Records - N.C. Gen. Stat. § 132-9

Any person who is denied access to public records for the purposes of inspection or examination, and any person who is denied copies of public records, may bring a civil action in court against the government agency or official who is denying access or copies. Courts are required to set public records suits for immediate hearings, and give hearings of these cases priority over other cases. The court may order the agency to permit inspection or provide copies if the court determines that the person seeking the records is entitled to them.

If a person files a civil action and succeeds in having the judge order the inspection or copying of public records, the court may also order the agency to pay the successful party's attorney's fees. The court may order the payment of attorney's fees against a public agency if it finds that the agency acted without substantial justification in denying access to the public records and there are no special circumstances that would make the award of attorney's fees unjust.

Attorneys' fees assessed against a public agency are charged against the operating expenses of the agency. However, the court may order an individual public official or employee to pay all or part of the attorneys' fees if that person knowingly or intentionally violated the law. Attorneys' fees may not be assessed against public officials or employees who sought and followed the advice of an attorney regarding the disclosure or copying of the records in question.

A court may order the person who brought a public records lawsuit to pay attorneys' fees to the public agency if the court determines that the lawsuit was frivolous or was brought in bad faith.

In two cases the North Carolina courts discussed the circumstances in which attorney's fees should be awarded against public agencies in public records lawsuits.

In *North Carolina Press Asso. v. Spangler*, 87 N.C. App. 169, 360 S.E.2d 138 (1987), the North Carolina Court of Appeals said attorney's fees may be awarded unless the government agency has substantial justification in withholding them, and the government agency has the burden of proving that it had substantial justification. In *S.E.T.A. UNC-CH, INC. v. Huffines*, 107 N.C. App. 440, 420 S.E.2d 674 (1992), the Court of Appeals said the test for substantial justification is not whether the court ultimately finds the agency's reasons for resisting public disclosure to be correct - the test is whether a reasonable person could think the agency was correct, given the existing law and facts.

In *Spangler*, the Court found that the agency lacked substantial justification for resisting disclosure and the attorney's fees award was upheld (the agency argued that it was justified in withholding disclosure because the disputed documents were preliminary working papers and intergovernmental communications which the agency believed should be exempted from the public records law). In *Huffines*, the Court rejected an attorney's fee award, finding that although the disputed documents should have been released the agency had substantial justification in believing the documents should be withheld (the agency argued that releasing the disputed documents - university research grant applications - would have a chilling effect on university research and academic freedom).

A person who has been denied access to public records must bring a separate civil action to gain access. A violation of the public records law's disclosure requirements cannot be asserted as an affirmative defense in another suit. In *Housing Authority of Raleigh v. Montgomery*, 55 N.C. App. 422, 286 S.E.2d 114 (1982), a housing authority brought condemnation proceedings to obtain privately owned land. The landowner asked the housing authority for copies of appraisals it had done for her land, and the authority refused to provide them. As part of her defense to the condemnation proceeding, the landowner claimed that the housing authority violated the public records law by failing to provide her with the appraisals. The North Carolina Court of Appeals ruled that the landowner could not assert a violation of the public records law as an affirmative defense in a condemnation proceeding. The Court said that the proper procedure for compelling disclosure of the documents would have been a separate action under N.C. Gen. Stat. § 132-9.

Certain Government Records are Exempt from Disclosure

The public records law exempts certain types of records from required disclosure. The law says that records containing certain communications between attorneys and their government clients,[14] State tax information,[15] trade secrets,[16] certain lawsuit settlements,[17] criminal investigation records,[8] and records about industrial expansion[19] are not public records and are not subject to public disclosure requirements. These exemptions are discussed in detail in Part II of this manual, which also contains the public records exemptions found in other sections of the North Carolina General Statutes.

N.C. Gen. Stat. § 132-1.1(a)

N.C. Gen. Stat. § 132-1.1(b)

N.C. Gen. Stat. § 132-1.2

N.C. Gen. Stat. § 132-1.3

N.C. Gen. Stat. § 132-1.4

N.C. Gen. Stat. § 132-6

The Open Meetings Law

Meetings of Public Bodies to be Conducted Openly (Public Policy) - N.C. Gen. Stat. § 143-318.9

The North Carolina General Assembly has declared the following public policy on meetings of public bodies:

> "Whereas the public bodies that administer the legislative, policy-making, quasi-judicial, administrative and advisory functions of North Carolina and its political subdivisions exist solely to conduct the people's business, it is the public policy of North Carolina that the hearings, deliberations, and actions of these bodies be conducted publicly."

In *Jacksonville Daily News Co. v. Onslow County Bd. of Educ.*, 113 N.C. App. 127, 439 S.E.2d 607 (1993), the North Carolina Court of Appeals ruled that a school board's deliberations before giving itself retroactive pay raises were the kinds of "deliberations" and "actions" that should be conducted openly at a public meeting. The Court ruled that the board violated the open meetings law when it considered and granted retroactive pay raises for its members in closed sessions and private telephone conversations among board members.

Official Meetings of Public Bodies are Open to the Public - N.C. Gen. Stat. § 143-318.10(a)

Each official meeting of a public body must be open to the public, and any person is entitled to attend an official meeting.

Public Bodies Defined - N.C. Gen. Stat. § 143-318.10(b) and (c)

Groups that are required to hold their official meetings publicly ("public bodies") include government authorities, boards, commissions, committees, councils, or other bodies. The law applies to all these bodies of the State, or of one or more counties, cities, school administrative units, constituent institutions of the University of North Carolina, or other political subdivisions or public corporations in the State.

These groups are public bodies if they have two or more members, if their members are elected or appointed, and if they exercise a legislative, policy-making, quasi-judicial, administrative, or advisory function.

In *Winfas Inc. v. Region P Human Dev. Agency,* 64 N.C. App. 724, 308 S.E.2d 99 (1983), the North Carolina Court of Appeals held that the fact that a human development agency created by a county later became a nonprofit corporation did not alter its status as a public body for the purposes of the open meetings law.

In *Northampton County Drainage Dist. Number One v. Bailey,* 92 N.C. App. 68, 373 S.E.2d 560 (1988), the North Carolina Court of Appeals ruled that a drainage district was a political subdivision of the State with quasi-judicial and administrative authority, and it was therefore a public body subject to the meeting notice provisions of the open meetings law.

Official Meetings Defined - N.C. Gen. Stat. § 143-318.10(e)

Public bodies are required to allow the public to attend their official meetings. An official meeting is a meeting, assembly, or gathering together of a majority of the members of a public body for the purpose of conducting hearings, participating in deliberations, voting upon public business, or otherwise transacting public business. It does not matter when or where a meeting occurs - if a majority of the public body's members get together for one of these purposes it is an official meeting. Meetings held by telephone conference call or other electronic means are official meetings.

Social gatherings or other informal assemblies of public body members are not official meetings if public business is not discussed or considered. Members of public bodies may not hold a social gathering to evade the spirit and purposes of the open meetings law.

Public Notice of Official Meetings - N.C. Gen. Stat. § 143-318.12

The open meetings law contains detailed procedures that public bodies must follow to give the public advance notice of their official meetings. Requirements differ depending on whether the official meeting is a regular meeting, a meeting other than a regular meeting, or an emergency meeting.[20]

Regular Meetings

A public body is not required to set up a schedule of regular meetings. However, if a public body does make a schedule of regular meetings it is required to keep a copy of that schedule on file with a clerk or secretary. The schedule should show the time and place of the regular meetings. (If meetings are held by conference call or other electronic means, the notice should say where the public may go to listen). The schedule must be kept on file, depending on the nature of the public body, as follows:

1) For public bodies that are part of State government, the schedule should be kept on file with the Secretary of State;

Some of the notice requirements discussed here differ slightly for meetings and hearings of city and town councils (See, N.C. Gen. Stat. § 160A-71) and meetings and hearings of boards of county commissioners (See, N.C. Gen. Stat. § 153A-40). These differences are discussed in Part II of this manual.

2) For governing boards and other public bodies of county government, the schedule should be kept on file with the clerk of the board of the county commissioners;

3) For governing boards and other public bodies of city or town government, the schedule should be kept on file with the city or town clerk; and

4) For all other public bodies, the schedule should be kept on file with its clerk or secretary. If the public body does not have a clerk or secretary, the schedule should be kept on file with the clerk to the board of county commissioners in the county where the public body normally holds its meetings.

If a public body changes its schedule of regular meetings, it is required to file the revised schedule with the clerk or secretary as indicated above. The revised schedule must be filed at least seven calendar days before the next meeting to be held under the revised schedule.

Sometimes a public body adjourns or recesses one of its regularly scheduled meetings and agrees to continue the meeting at a different time or place. If the public body, during the regular meeting, announces the time and place for the continuation of the meeting, then the public body is not required to give any other notice of the time and place of the continued meeting. If the public body does not announce the time and place of a continued meeting during the regularly scheduled meeting, the public body must give an extra notice of the continued meeting as discussed immediately below in "Meetings Other than Regular Meetings."

Meetings Other than Regular Meetings

Sometimes public bodies do not meet according to a regular schedule. If they do not do so, they must give public notice of their meetings according to the following requirements. (These requirements also apply to the continuation of a recessed or adjourned regular meeting if the time and place of the continued meeting is not announced during the regular meeting).

The public body must make a written notice giving the time, place and purpose of its next meeting. The public body must post this notice on its principal bulletin board (if the public body does not have a bulletin board it must post the notice at the door of its usual meeting room). The notice must be posted at least 48 hours before the meeting.[21]

In *Wright v. County of Macon,* 64 N.C. App. 718, 308 S.E.2d 97 (1983), the North Carolina Court of Appeals ruled that a county board of commissioners complied with N.C. Gen. Stat. § 143-318.12 by posting notice on August 13 that a regular meeting,

In addition to posting the notice for these meetings, the public body must offer the media and the public the opportunity to put themselves on a list of people or organizations to be notified of all these meetings. Those who want to receive meeting notices may file written requests for notice with the clerk, secretary or some other person designated by the public body. The public body may require newspapers, wire services, radio stations, and television stations to renew these written requests annually. For all other people or organizations, the public body may require them to renew their requests quarterly and must charge them a ten-dollar annual fee to be placed on the list of people to receive meeting notices.

If a media organization, person, or other organization has submitted a written request to be notified of the public body's unscheduled official meetings, the public body must mail or deliver a notice of these meetings to the person or organization at least 48 hours before the meeting.

Emergency Meetings

Sometimes public bodies hold emergency meetings. A meeting is an emergency meeting if it is called because of generally unexpected circumstances that require immediate consideration by the public body.

As discussed above, public bodies must give media and other members of the public the opportunity to submit written requests for notification of unscheduled meetings. For emergency meetings, the public body is required to give notice to some, but not necessarily all, of the organizations and people who have submitted requests. For emergency meetings, the public body is required to give notice of the meeting to each *local* newspaper, wire service, radio station and television station that has filed with the public body a written request for notice and which has included its telephone number for emergency notice.

For all local media that qualify for notice of emergency meetings, the public body must give them notice of the meeting either by telephone or by the same method used to notify the members of the public body of the meeting. This notice must be given to these qualifying media immediately after notice is given to the members of the public body. The expense of the notice must be paid for by the notified party.

At an emergency meeting, a public body may only consider business connected with the emergency.

Open Meetings Law Only Guarantees the Public's Right to Attend Official Meetings

All people and media have the right to attend official meetings of public bodies.

---

which was adjourned on August 2, would be reconvened on August 16.

N.C. Gen. Stat. 143-318.10(a). However, the open meetings law does not give members of the public the right to speak or participate in an official meeting.[22]

In fact, if a person interrupts, disturbs, or disrupts an official meeting, the presiding officer may direct that person to leave the meeting. If that happens and the disruptive person refuses to leave, he may be charged with a misdemeanor. N.C. Gen. Stat. § 143-318.17.

Public's Right to Listen to Electronic Meetings - N.C. Gen. Stat. § 143-318.13(a)

A public body may hold a meeting by conference telephone or other electronic means. If it does so, it has to provide a location and means for members of the public to listen to the meeting. The meeting notice should indicate where the public may listen. The public body may charge up to twenty-five dollars to each listener to help pay for the cost of providing the location and listening equipment.

Public's Right to Record Official Meeting - N.C. Gen. Stat. § 143-318.14

Any person may photograph, film, tape-record, or otherwise reproduce any part of an official meeting required to be open.

Regulation of Broadcasting and Recording at Official Meetings - N.C. Gen. Stat. 143-318.14

Radio and television stations are entitled to broadcast all or any part of an official meeting required to be open.

A public body may regulate the placement and use of equipment necessary for broadcasting, photographing, filming, or recording a meeting. This applies to equipment used by the media and equipment used by private people.

The public body may regulate the use of broadcasting and recording equipment only to prevent undue interference with the meeting. The public body must allow broadcasting and recording equipment to be placed in the meeting room so the equipment may be used. The ordinary use of this equipment, by itself, may not be considered to be interference with the meeting.

If the meeting room is not big enough to accommodate all the members of the

---

There are other North Carolina laws that require certain government bodies to hold public hearings to consider certain public business. Some of these laws require that members of the public be allowed to speak at such hearings. However, the open meetings law deals only with the right to attend official meetings of public bodies.

public body, members of the public in attendance, and all the broadcasting and recording equipment and personnel without interfering with the meeting, *and* if an adequate alternative meeting room is not readily available, the public body may require the pooling of broadcasting/recording equipment and the people operating it. If the meeting room is not big enough and the news media request an alternate site for the meeting, the public body may move the meeting to the alternate site and may require that the media requesting the alternate site pay for any costs incurred in securing the alternate site.

In *Leak v. High Point City Council*, 25 N.C. App. 394, 213 S.E.2d 386 (1975) (a case decided before the enactment of N.C. Gen. Stat. § 143-318.14), the North Carolina Court of Appeals ruled that there was no justification for excluding live radio and television coverage of city council investigative hearings on police corruption.

Public Bodies May Not Conceal the Subject of their Actions or Deliberations - N.C. Gen. Stat. § 143-318.13(c)

If members of a public body deliberate, vote or take other action on a matter at an official meeting, they must do so in a way that allows the public in attendance to understand what subject is being considered. The members may not consider matters by reference to letters, numbers, or other secret devices or methods with the intention of making it impossible for the public to understand what they are considering.

The public body *may* deliberate, vote or take action by reference to an agenda if the agenda is worded so that the subjects to be considered can be understood and if copies of the agenda are available for public inspection at the meeting.

Public Bodies May Not Vote by Secret Ballot - N.C. Gen. Stat. 143-318.13(b)

Public bodies may not vote by secret ballot.

Public bodies may vote by written ballot, but only if the following requirements are met. Each member of the public body must sign his written ballot. The minutes of the meeting must show the vote of each member who votes. The written ballots must be made available for public inspection in the office of the public body's clerk or secretary immediately after the meeting in which the vote took place. The written ballots must be kept available for inspection in that office until the minutes of the meeting are approved. Only then may the written ballots be destroyed.

Emergency Meetings of Public Bodies - N.C. Gen. Stat. § 143-318.12(b)(3)

Public bodies may call emergency meetings if there are generally unexpected circumstances that require immediate consideration by the public body. At an emergency meeting, the public body may consider only the business connected with the emergency circumstances.

For a discussion of the special notice requirements for emergency meetings, see the section on Public Notice of Official Meetings, above.

Public Bodies Must Keep Minutes of Official Meetings - N.C. Gen. Stat. § 143-318.10(e)

Every public body is required to keep full and accurate minutes of all official meetings. Minutes may be kept in writing, or in the form of sound or video recordings. These minutes are public records, subject to public inspection and copying in accordance with the North Carolina public records law.

Public bodies are required to keep minutes of all portions of official meetings, including all closed sessions, which are held during official meetings. (See the section on Closed Sessions, below). Minutes of legitimate closed sessions are public records, but they may be withheld from public inspection so long as public inspection would frustrate the purpose of the closed session.

In *News & Observer Pub. Co. v. Poole*, 330 N.C. 465, 412 S.E.2d 7 (1992), the North Carolina Supreme Court ruled that government agencies not subject to the open meetings law may not claim that law's exemption for disclosure of minutes of closed sessions. The government commission in *Poole* was not a "public body" subject to the open meetings law. During one of its meetings, the commission's attorney provided legal advice to the commission, and his advice was recorded in the commission's minutes. A newspaper sought disclosure of those minutes. The commission argued that it should not have to disclose those portions of the minutes containing the legal advice, since the commission, had it been subject to the open meetings law, could have held a closed session to receive the legal advice.

The Court ruled that the commission's minutes were not entitled to the open meetings law's protection from disclosure because the commission was not subject to the open meetings law at all. The Court said, "Not being burdened by this law's provisions, the Commission is not entitled to its benefits."

Closed Sessions of Official Meetings - N.C. Gen. Stat. § 143-318.11

The open meetings law permits public bodies to exclude the public from certain portions of official meetings. These are referred to as closed sessions.[23]

Closed sessions are not unofficial meetings where members of public bodies may discuss anything they want and take any action they want out of the sight and

---

Before October 1994, these sessions were referred to in the law as executive sessions. Some public bodies, and even some parts of the North Carolina General Statutes, may still refer to these sessions as executive sessions.

hearing of the public. Closed sessions may be held only as part of an official meeting of a public body. The subjects that may be discussed and the actions that may be taken in closed sessions are listed specifically in the open meetings law, and only these things may be considered during a closed session. The business conducted at a closed session is still considered to be public business. The General Assembly has indicated that a public body should hold a closed session only for the purpose of acting in the public's interest.

Procedure for Holding a Closed Session - N.C. Gen. Stat. § 143-318.11(c)

The proper procedure for holding a closed session is as follows. A public body may hold a closed session only if it first begins an open official meeting after proper public notice. During the open part of the official meeting, the public body must make and adopt a motion to hold a closed session. In making the motion to hold a closed session the public body must state which of the legally acceptable purposes (as listed in the open meetings law at N.C. Gen. Stat. 143-318.11(a) it is relying upon to justify the closed session. (These reasons are listed and discussed, below).

Once the public body is in a closed session it must keep full and accurate minutes of that closed session. Although minutes of official meetings are public records, a public body is permitted to withhold its minutes of a closed session from public inspection so long as public inspection would frustrate the purpose of the closed session.

Permitted Purposes for Holding Closed Sessions - N.C. Gen. Stat. § 143-318.11(a)

The open meetings law says that a public body may hold a closed session during one of its official meetings only when a closed session is required to prevent public disclosure of the following seven types of information:

1. **Legally Confidential Information.**

    Certain information is made confidential or privileged by state or federal laws. (For example, patient medical information is confidential. So are trade secrets). Public bodies may hold closed sessions to prevent disclosure of information that is legally confidential or privileged or is not subject to the public records law.

    If a public body holds a closed session to prevent disclosure of this kind of information, when it makes the motion to hold the closed session it must state which law makes the information confidential or privileged.

2. **Honorary Degrees, Scholarships, Prizes and Awards**

    Public bodies may hold closed sessions to discuss honorary degrees, scholarships, prizes and awards so that these things will not be announced prematurely.

3. **Attorney-Client Discussions**

The North Carolina General Assembly has acknowledged that there is an attorney-client privilege between public bodies and their attorneys.[24] A public body may hold a closed session to keep from revealing information and communications between the public body and its attorney, which are subject to the attorney-client privilege.

The open meetings law does not list all of the kinds of information that might be subject to the attorney-client privilege. However, the law specifies that a public body may hold an attorney-client closed session to consider and give instructions to an attorney on the handling or settlement of a claim, judicial action or administrative procedure. If the public body considers or approves a settlement in a closed session, the terms of that settlement must be reported publicly and entered into the public minutes of the body as soon as possible within a reasonable time after the settlement is concluded (this does *not* apply to settlements of malpractice claims by or on behalf of hospitals).[25]

A public body may not hold a closed session simply because its attorney is present or is a participant in the discussion. The public body may hold the closed session only if it is necessary to discuss information that is truly subject to the attorney-client privilege. Once it is in a closed session, the public body may not discuss general policy matters.

If a public body holds a closed session to receive advice from its attorney about an existing lawsuit or lawsuits, when the motion is made to

---

In *News & Observer Pub. Co. v. Poole*, 330 N.C. 465, 412 S.E.2d 7 (1992) the North Carolina Supreme Court said that it had not yet determined whether such a privilege existed for government agencies. The General Assembly responded to this in 1994 amendments to the open meetings law, saying that the attorney-client privilege between attorneys and public bodies "is hereby acknowledged." N.C. Gen. Stat. § 143-318.11(a)(3)

In *Moore v. Beaufort County*, 936 F.2d 159 (4th Cir. 1991), the U.S. Court of Appeals for the 4th Circuit ruled that a county board's closed session instructions to their attorney to settle a lawsuit gave the attorney binding authority to resolve the suit, and his subsequent settlement was binding on the board. No formal approval of the settlement by the board in a subsequent open session was required before the board could be bound by the agreement. All the open meetings law required was that the settlement terms be entered into the board's minutes in a later open session.

hold the closed session the public body must state the names of the parties in the lawsuit.

4. **Location or Expansion of Businesses**

   A public body may hold a closed session to discuss matters related to the location or expansion of industries or other businesses in the area served by the public body.

5. **Contract Negotiations**

   A public body may hold a closed session to establish negotiating positions, or to instruct its staff or agents about negotiating positions, to be taken on certain types of contracts. In a closed session the public body may consider and discuss negotiating positions on: 1) the price or other material terms of contracts to acquire real property by purchase, option, exchange or lease; and 2) the amount of compensation and other material terms of employment contracts.

6. **Certain Personnel Matters**

   A public body may hold a closed session in limited circumstances to consider certain personnel matters regarding individual employees or prospective employees. In a closed session, a public body may consider the qualifications, competence, performance, character, fitness, conditions of appointment, or conditions of initial employment of a current or prospective public employee or officer. In a closed session a public body may also hear or investigate a complaint, charge or grievance by or against an individual public employee or officer.

   A public body may not remain in closed session to take any final action regarding these personnel matters. A public body must be in open session in an official meeting to take final action on the appointment, discharge or removal of employees or officers.

   These provisions permitting public bodies to hold closed sessions regarding personnel matters apply only to employees and officers. They do not apply to members of the public body, itself, or members of other public bodies. A public body may not hold a closed session to consider the qualifications, competence, performance, character, fitness, appointment or removal of one of its own members or members of any other public body. A public body may not hold a closed session to consider or fill a vacancy among its own membership or the membership of other public bodies. All of these things must be considered and acted upon in open sessions.

A public body also is not permitted to consider general personnel policy issues in a closed session.

In a 1976 opinion the North Carolina Attorney General said that the State Personnel Commission may not use a closed session to deliberate upon and approve a county's plan to deviate from the Commission's standard salary ranges. 46 N.C.A.G. 20 (1976).

7. **Criminal Investigations**

A public body may hold closed sessions to hear reports about investigations, or to plan or conduct investigations, of alleged criminal misconduct.

Subjects No Longer Permitted in Closed Sessions

In 1994, the North Carolina General Assembly amended the open meetings law to eliminate several subjects from the list of purposes for which a public body may hold a closed session. Public bodies may no longer hold closed sessions to consider the following matters:

(1) Employment and discharge of independent contractors;

(2) Contingency plans for strikes and other work slowdowns;

(3) Handling riots and disorders;

(4) Correction system security problems;

(5) Airport landing fees;

(6) Personal property gifts and bequests;

(7) Acquiring artworks and artifacts; and

(8) Election irregularities.

Civil Actions for Violations of Open Meetings Law - N.C. Gen. Stat. § 143-318.16, § 143-318.16A, and § 143-318.16B

Any person may bring a civil court action against a public body for past violations or possible future violations of the open meetings law. Violations might include taking action or considering a matter other than at an official meeting, taking action or considering a matter at an unauthorized closed session, or failing to give proper notice of an official meeting.

If the person bringing a suit shows that the public body violated or is going to violate the open meetings law, the court may issue an injunction. An injunction may prohibit a threatened violation of the law, or prevent past violations of the law from recurring. N.C. Gen. Stat. § 143-318.16(a)

In a lawsuit under the open meetings law, the court may also declare that any action of a public body was taken, considered, discussed, or deliberated in violation of the law. If the court declares that an action or decision of a public body was taken in violation of the open meetings law, the court may also declare that the public body's action is null and void. N.C. Gen. Stat. § 143-318.16A(a).

In deciding whether to invalidate a public body's action for violating the open meetings law, a court considers these factors:

1) The extent to which the violation affected the substance of the challenged action;

2) The extent to which the violation thwarted or impaired access to meetings the public had a right to attend;

3) The extent to which the violation prevented or impaired public knowledge or understanding of the people's business;

4) Whether the violation was an isolated occurrence or part of a continuing pattern of violations;

5) The extent to which people relied on the validity of the challenged action, and the effect on those people of declaring the challenged action void; and

6) Whether the violation was committed in bad faith for the purpose of evading or subverting the public policy of the open meetings law.

N.C. Gen. Stat. § 143-318.16B(c)

If a person wants to bring a civil suit to have a court declare that a public body's action is null and void because it was taken in violation of the open meetings law, the person must file the suit within 45 days after the public body's action is first disclosed. This 45-day period for filing suit is counted from different dates, depending on the circumstances. If the public body's action is recorded in minutes of a meeting, then the 45-day period for filing suit begins on the date when the minutes are first made available for public inspection. If the public body's action is not recorded in minutes, then the 45-day period begins on the date when the person bringing the suit knew or should have known that the public body took the challenged action. N.C. Gen. Stat. § 143-318.16A(b)

There are different time limits for filing suit to challenge a public body's adoption of bond orders and bond referenda that are alleged to have been adopted in violation of the open meetings law. (N.C. Gen. Stat. § 143-318.16A(b) For a bond order, a suit must be filed within 30 days after the date of publication of the bond order as adopted. N.C. Gen. Stat. § 159-59 For a bond referendum, a suit must be filed within 30 days after the statement of the results of the referendum is published. N.C. Gen. Stat. § 159-62

When a suit is brought to challenge a public body action taken in violation of the open meetings law, the court may order the prevailing party to pay the attorney's fees of the losing party. This means that either the public body or the person filing the suit might be required to pay the other side's attorney's fees, depending upon who wins the suit and on whether the court decides that payment of attorney's fees is appropriate. If individual members of a public body are found to have violated the open meetings law knowingly or intentionally, the court may order those individual members to pay all or part of the challenger's attorney's fees. However, the court may not assess attorney's fees against individual members of a public body if the public body or those individual members sought the advice of an attorney in taking their action, and if they followed that advice. N.C. Gen. Stat. § 143-318.16B.

In suits challenging public body actions taken in violation of the open meetings law, courts are required to schedule hearings on those suits immediately and to give priority to these hearings. N.C. Gen. Stat. § 143-318.16C.

The North Carolina courts have interpreted the enforcement provisions of the open meetings law in several decisions.

In *Jacksonville Daily News Co. v. Onslow County Bd. of Educ.*, 113 N.C. App. 127, 439 S.E.2d 607 (1993), the North Carolina Court of Appeals determined that a judgment declaring a school board's actions in violation of the open meetings law was an appropriate remedy, when it was found that the school board considered and granted retroactive pay raises to its members in a closed session discussions and in private telephone conversations among board members. The Court upheld an award of attorney's fees to the newspaper. However, the Court said that no purpose would be served in voiding the board's action or requiring the board members to return the money.

In *Coulter v. (City of Newton)(Newton)*, 100 N.C. App. 523, 397 S.E.2d 244 (1990), the North Carolina Court of Appeals declined to nullify an allegedly improper closed session action by a city board. In *Coulter,* landowners challenged the city's permit for building a trailer park on land adjacent to theirs. The landowners claimed that the city aldermen, in a closed session, improperly reached an agreement with the trailer park owner in which the town committed itself to extend a waterline line to the park. The Court of Appeals said that even if the waterline commitment was made improperly during a closed session (which the court did not address), the board later held a public hearing on the subject of the trailer park permit and voted properly to extend the waterline. The Court ruled that the later hearing and vote cured any alleged impropriety occurring during the closed session.

In *Eggimann v. Wake County Board of Education*, 22 N.C. App. 459, 206 S.E.2d 754 (1974) (a case decided before the enactment of N.C. Gen. Stat. § 143-318.16A), the North Carolina Court of Appeals refused to rule that a school board's discussion in a private meeting of a school site selection was void. The Court noted that after the private discussion, the school board discussed the matter in a public meeting, and the final vote on site selection was also made in a public meeting. The Court also held that the private meetings of the school board did not violate constituents' constitutional rights of due process and equal protection.

In *Lewis v. White*, 287 S.E.2d 134, 287 N.C. 625 (1975), the North Carolina Supreme Court ruled that the wording of a request for injunctive relief sought by the plaintiff was inappropriate. The plaintiff sued an art museum building commission, claiming that they had made decisions and taken certain actions in secret, nonpublic meetings. The plaintiff asked the Court to enjoin the commission from performing its duties and exercising its authorities until "all of their meetings are held as open meetings." The Supreme Court said that would make it impossible for the commission to carry out its duties, because the commission could not demonstrate that all its meetings were open until after all the meetings were held and no more meetings were planned. The Court implied that a more appropriate request for relief might be a request for an order that the public be admitted to future meetings.

In *Northampton County Drainage Dist. Number One v. Bailey*, 92 N.C. App. 68, 373 S.E.2d 560 (1988), the North Carolina Court of Appeals addressed a claim that a drainage district's fee assessments violated landowners' due process rights because the district had not given proper notice of the meetings at which it assessed the fees. The Court found that the landowners had raised an open meetings law challenge to the district's action within 45 days, which the landowners could have done. N.C. Gen. Stat. § 143-318.16A. The Court ruled that since the landowners did not use the open meetings law to challenge the assessments, their due process challenge was without foundation.

In *Coulter v. (City of Newton)(Newton)*, 100 N.C. App. 523, 397 S.E.2d 244 (1990), the North Carolina Court of Appeals ruled that a suit challenging an allegedly improper action taken by a city board during a closed session was barred because the plaintiffs filed suit more than 45 days after the board's action was disclosed. The board's action at a closed session, which occurred in February 1987, was revealed to the plaintiffs for the first time at an open board session in June 1988. The plaintiffs filed their suit in September 1988, more than 60 days after the board's action was revealed.

In *Dockside Discotheque (, Inc.) v. Board of Adjustment (of the Town of Southern Pines)*, 115 N.C. App. 303, 444 S.E.2d 451 (1994), the North Carolina Court of Appeals held that a town board of adjustment's unauthorized closed session was not sufficient grounds to declare the board's later action null and void. A disco owner had asked the board for an exception to the town's development ordinance that would permit topless entertainment at the disco. The board considered the request at a public meeting. Before voting, the board went into closed session without a motion to do so, and without stating a reason for the closed session. Immediately after the closed session, the board, with no discussion, voted in open session to deny the request.

The disco owner sued the board, alleging that the closed session violated the open meetings law. He asked the court to declare the board's action null and void.

The Court of Appeals said a decision whether to declare a public body's action null and void based on an open meeting law violation is discretionary. The Court held that since the board's closed session had little effect on the substance of their decision, the Court would not declare their final action null and void.

Certain Groups Are Subject/Not Subject to the Open Meetings Law

The open meetings law specifies several public agencies or organizations that are either subject or not subject to the law. For a listing of the groups mentioned specifically in the open meetings law, see the following sections in Part II: Public Hospital Boards - N.C. Gen. Stat. § 143-318.10(b); Government Bodies Not Subject to the Open Meetings Law - N.C. Gen. Stat. §§ 143-318.10(c) and 143-318.18; and Legislative Commissions, Committees and Standing Subcommittees - N.C. Gen. Stat. § 14A.

Part II
Exceptions, Modifications, and References to Public Records and Open Meetings in the North Carolina General Statutes

There are many exceptions to the public records and open meetings laws. Some of these are listed in the two laws, themselves. Many more are found in other sections of the North Carolina General Statutes dealing directly with the government agency or program to which they apply.

In some cases, certain records and meetings are completely exempt from public access requirements. In other cases, access is limited to certain people or in certain situations. In addition to these exceptions, many sections of the North Carolina General Statutes simply confirm that certain records are public and certain meetings are open.

All of these exceptions and references are listed and discussed Part II. For the most part, these exceptions and references are listed here in the numerical order they appear in the General Statutes. In a few instances, scattered sections that deal with the same subject are grouped together for convenience and to avoid repetition. For example, the General Statutes contain nine separate sections dealing with the confidentiality of personnel records of various types of government agencies. For convenience, they are listed and discussed together. (See, Personnel Records of Government Employees - N.C. Gen. Stat. § 126-22. etc.)

Readers who are interested in finding exceptions or references by subject or agency should refer to the alphabetical Index to this manual. Court decisions and Attorney General opinions are mentioned in these sections as relevant subjects are discussed.

Courts Shall Be Open - N.C. Const., Art. I, § 18

The North Carolina Constitution requires that courts should be open.

In two cases, *In re Norwell*, 293 N.C. 235, 237 S.E.2d 246 (1977), and *In re Peoples*, 296 N.C. 109, 250 S.E.2d 890 (1978), judges were censured for disposing of cases out of court.

Arbitral Tribunals N.C. Gen. Stat. § 1-567.54(d)

Proceedings of arbitral tribunals may be conducted through oral hearings or on the basis of written documents. Unless the parties agree otherwise, oral hearings must be held in camera (privately, before a judge). Confidential information disclosed during the proceedings may not be divulged by the arbitrator. Unless otherwise agreed by the parties, or required by applicable law, the arbitral tribunal and the parties must keep confidential all matters relating to the arbitration and the award.

Discovery in Civil Actions - Protective Orders - N.C. Gen. Stat. § 1A-1, Rule 26(c)

In civil actions, a judge may issue a protective order requiring that information obtained through discovery be sealed (not publicly disclosed). The judge may do this upon the motion of any party or a person from whom discovery is sought. A judge may issue a protective order to protect the party or person from unreasonable annoyance, embarrassment, oppression, or undue burden or expense. Judges have specific authority to order that trade secrets or other confidential research, development or commercial information not be disclosed.

Medical Records Subpoenaed in Civil Actions - N.C. Gen. Stat. § 1A-1(c)

Medical records subpoenaed in civil actions are not open to inspection or copying by anyone except the parties to the case and their attorneys until the judge orders that they be published. This provision does not waive the physician-client privilege (See, N.C. Gen. Stat. §8-53).

Removal of District Attorneys - N.C. Gen. Stat. § 7A-66

Court hearings for the suspension or removal of district attorneys are open to the public.

Clerks of Superior Court - Court Records - N.C. Gen. Stat. § 7A-109

Clerks of superior court in each county keep records, files, dockets and indexes as required by the Administrative Office of the Courts, including records of civil actions, special proceedings, estates, criminal actions, juvenile actions, minutes of the court, judgments, liens, lis pendens and other records required by law to be kept.

Except as prohibited by law, these records are open to the inspection of the public during regular office hours.

Suspension, Removal, and Reinstatement of Magistrates - N.C. Gen. Stat. § 7A-173

Hearings for the suspension, removal or reinstatement of magistrates are open to the public.

Gag Orders - Courts May Not Issue Gag Orders on Public Records - N.C. Gen. Stat. § 7A-276.1

No court may prohibit or restrict the publication or broadcast of the contents of any public record.

Censure or Removal of Judges - N.C. Gen. Stat. § 7A-377

The Judicial Standards Commission investigates complaints about the qualifications or conduct of justices and judges. The Commission may investigate complaints, may hold formal proceedings, and may recommend to the North Carolina Supreme Court that judges or justices be censured or removed.

All papers filed with the Commission in these proceedings, and the proceedings themselves, are confidential unless the judge waives confidentiality.

However, after a preliminary investigation is completed, if the Commission institutes formal proceedings the notice and complaint filed by the Commission, along with the answer and other pleadings, are not confidential. Formal hearings ordered by the Commission are not confidential. Recommendations of the Commission to the Supreme Court, and the record filed in support of the recommendations, are also not confidential.

Investigations of Child Abuse, Neglect or Dependency - N.C. Gen. Stat. § 7A-544

Departments of Social Services investigate reports of child abuse, neglect, or dependency. All information obtained by the Department of Social Services in these investigations is to be held in the strictest of confidence.

Central Registry of Child Abuse, Neglect and Dependency Cases - N.C. Gen. Stat. § 7A-552

The Department of Human Resources keeps a central registry of child abuse, neglect, and dependency cases, and child fatalities due to maltreatment. The data are confidential, subject to policies adopted by the Social Services Commission. The data may not be used at any hearing or court proceeding unless based upon a final judgment of a court of law.

Information Obtained by Guardians Ad Litem in Child Abuse and Neglect Cases - N.C. Gen. Stat. § 7A-586

In child abuse and neglect cases, guardians ad litem may be given authority by judges to collect information or reports, whether confidential or not, which are relevant to the case. Neither the physician-client privilege nor the husband-wife privilege may be used to prevent a guardian ad litem from obtaining this information. However, a guardian ad litem is required to respect the confidentiality of the information and make no disclosure of it to anyone except by order of the judge or as otherwise provided for by law.

Juveniles

Probable Cause Hearings for Juveniles 14 and Older - N.C. Gen. Stat. § 7A-609

When a juvenile 14 years or older is alleged to have committed a felony, the judge conducts a hearing to determine probable cause, unless the juvenile waives the hearing. The judge may exclude the public from this hearing unless the juvenile moves that the hearing be open.

Adjudicatory Hearings for Juveniles - N.C. Gen. Stat. § 7A-629

A judge may exclude the public from a juvenile's adjudicatory hearing unless the juvenile moves that the hearing be open.

Dispositional Hearings for Juveniles - N.C. Gen. Stat. § 7A-640

A judge may exclude the public from a juvenile's dispositional hearing unless the juvenile moves that the hearing be open.

Juvenile Delinquency Records in the Hands of Division of Youth Services - N.C. Gen. Stat. § 7A-652

When delinquent juveniles are placed with the Division of Youth Services, the Division may obtain a variety of records relating to those juveniles. The Division must maintain the confidentiality of those records that are legally confidential.

Review Hearings for Juvenile Placements After Termination of Parental Rights - N.C. Gen. Stat. § 7A-659

Courts hold periodic hearings to review placements of juveniles whose parents have had their parental rights terminated. These hearings are open only to the child (if he is at least 12 years old), the legal custodian of the child, the foster parent, and the guardian ad litem, except as otherwise directed by the court.

Confidentiality of Juvenile Records - N.C. Gen. Stat. § 7A-675

The clerk of superior court keeps a confidential record of all juvenile cases filed in the clerk's office. This record includes summonses, petitions, custody orders, court orders, written motions, recordings of hearings, and other papers filed in the proceeding.[26] This record must be withheld from public inspection and may be examined only by order of the judge, except that the juvenile, his parent, guardian, custodian, or other authorized representative of the juvenile have a right to examine the juvenile's record.

The chief court counselor keeps records of the cases of all juveniles under court counselor supervision. These records may be examined only by order of the judge, except that the juvenile may inspect them.

The Department of Social Services keeps records of cases of juveniles under protective custody by the Department or under placement by the court. These records may be examined only by order of the judge, except that the juvenile may inspect them.

Law enforcement records concerning juveniles are open only to the inspection of the prosecutor, court counselors, the juvenile, his parents, guardian and custodian.

Records on juveniles kept by the Division of Youth Services must be withheld from public inspection and are open only to the inspection by the juvenile, professionals in that agency who are directly involved in that juvenile's case, and court counselors. The judge authorizing commitment of a juvenile may inspect and order the release of these records.

Disclosure of information about any juvenile under investigation or alleged to be within the jurisdiction of the court that would reveal the identity of that juvenile is prohibited, except that publication of pictures of runaways is allowed with the permission of the parents.

In a 1988 opinion the North Carolina Attorney General said that law enforcement officers must forward collision investigation reports involving juveniles to the Division of Motor Vehicles, pursuant to N.C. Gen. Stat. § 20-166.1(e). Collision reports, in and of themselves, do not contain allegations of criminal offenses by juveniles. 58 N.C.A.G. 33 (1988).

Expunction of Records of Delinquent and Undisciplined Juveniles - N.C. Gen. Stat. § 7A-676

Juveniles who have been adjudicated delinquent or undisciplined may, when

---

In a 1975 opinion the North Carolina Attorney General said that juvenile arrest records are included in this confidential record. 44 N.C.A.G. 305 (1975).

they reach 16, petition the court for expunction of their records for misdemeanors and less serious felonies.

Juveniles may also, at age 16, petition the court for expunction of records of dismissed allegations that they were delinquent or undisciplined.

Expunction of Juvenile Criminal Convictions - N.C. Gen. Stat. § 15A-145(d)

In certain circumstances, people under 18 may have criminal convictions expunged from court records. The Administrative Office of the Courts keeps a file that lists people whose convictions have been expunged in accordance with this section. This file is confidential, and information in the file may only be disclosed to judges for the purpose of finding out whether a person charged with an offense was granted an expungement.

In a 1979 opinion the North Carolina Attorney General said that these expunction provisions apply to juvenile adjudications in which several misdemeanor charges were consolidated for trial and judgment. 49 N.C.A.G. 17 (1979).

Employment Discrimination Charges Investigated by Office of Administrative Hearings - N.C. Gen. Stat. § 7A-759(g)

The Office of Administrative Hearings (OAH) investigates employment discrimination complaints which are filed by State and local employees, and which are deferred to OAH by the U.S. Equal Employment Opportunity Commission. The standards of confidentiality established by federal statute or regulation for discrimination charges apply to deferred cases investigated or heard by OAH.

Privileged Communications

Communications Between Physician and Patient - N.C. Gen. Stat. § 8-53

Information obtained by licensed physicians in attending patients professionally, and which information is necessary for the physician to treat or prescribe for the patient, is not a public record. Physicians are not required to divulge any of this information. Confidential information contained in medical records may be furnished only on the authorization of the patient, or if deceased, the executor, administrator, or next of kin. However, subject to N.C. Gen. Stat. § 8-53.6, a judge or the Industrial Commission may require disclosure if it is necessary for the proper administration of justice.

In *State v. Shaw*, 305 N.C. 327, 289 S.E.2d 325 (1982), the North Carolina Supreme Court ruled that the physician-patient privilege does not apply to communications between optometrists and their patients.

Physician-Patient Privilege Waived in Child Abuse Cases - N.C. Gen. Stat. § 8-53.1

The physician-patient privilege is not grounds for excluding evidence regarding the abuse or neglect of a child under 16 years of age.

Communications Between Clergy and Communicants - N.C. Gen. Stat. § 8-53.2

Clergy are not competent to testify about information communicated to them by people seeking spiritual counsel or advice unless the communicant gives permission for the testimony.

Communications Between Psychologist and Client or Patient - N.C. Gen. Stat. § 8-53.3

Neither licensed psychologists nor psychological associates, or any of their employees, may be required to disclose any information which they acquired in the practice of psychology and which information was necessary to enable them to practice psychology. However, a judge may require disclosure if in the judge's opinion disclosure is necessary for the proper administration of justice.

School Counselor Privilege - N.C. Gen. Stat. § 8-53.4

No certified school counselor is competent to testify in any proceeding concerning information acquired in providing counseling to a student. However, a judge may require disclosure if in the judge's opinion disclosure is necessary to the proper administration of justice. A student may waive this privilege in court.

In a 1973 opinion the North Carolina Attorney General said that investigation papers compiled by school counselors are privileged records. 42 N.C.A.G. 229 (1973).

Communications Between Marital and Family Therapist and Client - N.C. Gen. Stat. § 8-53.5

No certified marital and family therapists, or any of their employees or associates, may be required to disclose any information which they acquired in providing professional marital and family therapy services. However, a judge may require disclosure in the interest of the proper administration of justice.

Marital Counseling Information in Alimony and Divorce Actions - N.C. Gen. Stat. § 8-53.6

In alimony and divorce actions, professionals providing marital counseling are not competent to testify concerning information acquired while providing counseling.

Social Worker Privilege - N.C. Gen. Stat. § 8-53.7

No certified social worker is required to disclose any information acquired in providing professional social work services. However, a judge may require disclosure if necessary for the proper administration of justice if disclosure is not prohibited by another statute or regulation.

Counselor Privilege - N.C. Gen. Stat. § 8-53.8

No licensed counselor is required to disclose information acquired in providing professional counseling services. However, a judge may require disclosure if necessary for the proper administration of justice if disclosure is not prohibited by some other statute or regulation.

Husband and Wife as Witness in Civil Actions - N.C. Gen. Stat. § 8-56

The husband or wife of a party to a civil action is competent to testify and may be required to give evidence, as any other witness on behalf of any party to the suit, except that no husband or wife may be required to disclose any confidential communication made by one to the other during their marriage.

Husband and Wife as Witness in Criminal Action - N.C. Gen. Stat. § 8-57

The spouse of a criminal defendant is competent to testify, but may not be required to testify for the State against the defendant in any criminal action or grand jury proceeding, except that the spouse may be required to testify in certain proceedings involving crimes against the spouse or the couple's children. However, in no event may a husband or wife be required to disclose any confidential communication made by one to the other during their marriage.

Records of Hearings into Past Sexual Behavior of Rape Victims - N.C. Gen. Stat. § 8C-1, RULE 412

In a rape or sexual offense criminal case, the sexual behavior of a complainant is considered relevant and admissible as evidence only in limited circumstances. Before evidence of any the complainant's sexual behavior may be presented in court, the judge must hold an in camera (private) hearing to determine whether the evidence will be allowed. The record of this in camera hearing and all evidence relating to it is open to inspection only by the parties, the complainant, their attorneys and the court and its agents. It may be used only as necessary for appellate review.

Jury Lists - N.C. Gen. Stat. §§ 9-2.1 and 9-4

Each county's register of deeds keeps a list of potential jurors. This list consists of potential juror information listed alphabetically, by juror, on separate cards. This list is available for public inspection during regular office hours.

In some counties, jury lists are kept on electronic data processing equipment instead of cards. The procedure for maintaining the lists must be in writing and must be available for public inspection.

When electronic data processing equipment is used to keep jury lists, the equipment may be used to sort juror names for random juror selection. Public access is limited to an alphabetical listing of the names. Access to the randomized list is prohibited.

Abortion Data Collected by Department of Human Resources - N.C. Gen. Stat. § 14-45.1

To compile statistical and demographic data on abortions, the Department of Human Resources collects reports on an annual basis from hospitals and clinics where abortions are performed. The reports submitted to the Department are for statistical purposes only and the confidentiality of the patient relationship is protected.

Probation Officers' Records; Parole Records - N.C. Gen. Stat. § 15-207

All information and data obtained by probation officers in carrying out their duties is privileged, and may not be disclosed to anyone other than a judge or others entitled to receive reports, unless disclosure is ordered by a judge or the Secretary of Correction.

Similarly, records compiled by the Department of Correction and the Parole Commission impacting on the possible parole of prisoners is confidential, and prisoners do not have a right to inspect files containing this information. *Goble v. Bounds*, 281 N.C. 307, 188 S.E.2d 347 (1972).

In *Paine v. Baker*, 595 F.2d 197 (4th Cir. N.C. 1979),*cert. denied*, 444 U.S. 925, 100 S. Ct. 263, 62 L.Ed.2d 181 (1979), the U.S. Court of Appeals for the Fourth Circuit confirmed that there is no general right of access to prison records. However, the Court ruled that a prisoner has a limited right of access to his prison records if there is a false item in his file and that information is relied on in a way that violates the prisoner's constitutional rights.

In *Carnahan v. Reed* 53 N.C. App. 589, 281 S.E.2d 408 (1981), a woman whose husband committed suicide in prison sought prison records of psychiatric evaluations performed on her husband. Department of Corrections rules restricted the release of prisoner psychiatric records to inmates, their doctors, or official personal representatives of deceased prisoners. The North Carolina Court of Appeals ruled that the prisoner's widow was not entitled to see the records because she had not been appointed officially as his legal representative. The Court also ruled that the widow did not have any property rights in the records.

Expunction of Criminal Charges N.C. Gen. Stat. § 15A-146

When criminal charges are dismissed, or when a criminal defendant is found not guilty, the person charged may apply for expunction of records relating to his or her apprehension or trial. The Administrative Office of the Courts keeps a file that lists people whose records have been expunged in accordance with this section. This file is confidential, and information in the file may only be disclosed to judges for the purpose of finding out whether a person charged with an offense was granted an expungement.

DNA Database - N.C. Gen. Stat. §§ 15A-266.12 and 15A-266.10

The State Bureau of Investigation collects and stores DNA profiles from people convicted of certain felonies. The profiles are kept for the purpose of assisting in future law enforcement efforts. The SBI may exchange this information with other specified law enforcement agencies for law enforcement purposes. This information is otherwise treated as confidential.

Any person whose DNA profiles are stored by the SBI may petition the court for expungement of those records if his felony conviction was reversed and the case dismissed.

Grand Jury Proceedings - N.C. Gen. Stat. § 15A-623

Grand jury proceedings are secret, and only specific people involved in those proceedings may attend.

A judge presiding at a grand jury may direct that a bill of indictment be kept secret until the defendant is arrested or appears before the court.

The name of a person subpoenaed to appear before an investigative grand jury, and the fact that he has been subpoenaed, may not be disclosed except by the person subpoenaed.

Grand jurors or others allowed to be present at grand jury proceedings may not disclose matters occurring at the proceedings. If they do so, they are in contempt of court.

Discovery in Criminal Cases - Information Not Otherwise Discoverable is Not Obtainable through the Public Records Law - N.C. Gen. Stat. § 15A, Article 48

Article 48 of Chapter 15A of the General Statutes regulates and limits the information defendants may obtain from the State through discovery in criminal prosecutions. In *Piedmont Publishing Co. v. City of Winston-Salem*, 334 N.C. 595, 434 S.E.2d 176 (1993), the North Carolina Supreme Court ruled that neither a criminal defendant nor the public may get any information through the public records law that the defendant could not get through the criminal discovery statute.

In 1994, following the decision in *Piedmont Publishing,* the General Assembly amended the public records law to say specifically that law enforcement agencies are not required to disclose any information that would not be required to be disclosed under the criminal procedure laws. N.C. Gen. Stat. § 132-1.4(h)(˙).

Discovery in Criminal Cases - Protective Orders - N.C. Gen. Stat. § 15A-908

In criminal cases, a judge may restrict the discovery or inspection of materials. The judge may do so for good cause, including a substantial risk to any person of physical harm, intimidation, bribery, economic reprisals, or unnecessary annoyance or embarrassment.

In *In re Investigation by Attorney General* (In re Southern Bell Tel. & Tel. Co.), 30 N.C. App. 585, 227 S.E.2d 645 (1976), the North Carolina Attorney General did an investigation into the possible misuse of funds by a corporation. In the investigation, the Attorney General got statements from employees through discovery. The North Carolina Court of Appeals ruled that the trial court properly imposed a protective order prohibiting the public disclosure of these employee statements prior to prosecution. The Court of Appeals said the justification for the protective order was the employees' personal right of privacy.

Reports on Incapacity of Criminal Defendants to Proceed with Trial - N.C. Gen. Stat. § 15A-1002

In determining whether a criminal defendant has the capacity to proceed with trial, a court may receive reports from medical experts on the defendant's capacity. These reports are not public records until introduced into evidence. Until these reports become public records, disclosure of their contents is limited to the prosecution and the defense, or as directed by the court.

Presentence Reports - N.C. Gen. Stat. § 15A-1333

Written presentence reports and records of oral presentence reports in criminal proceedings are not public records and may not be made available to anyone except the defendant, the defendant's attorney, the prosecutor or the court.

Crime Victim Compensation - Reports - N.C. Gen. Stat. § 15B-6

When investigating to determine compensation for crime victims, the director of the Crime Victims Compensation Commission may collect information from law enforcement agencies, State agencies and medical professionals. This information is subject to the same privilege against public disclosure that may be asserted by the providing source.

Crime Victim Compensation - Privilege and Records of Compensation Commission - N.C. Gen. Stat. § 15B-8.1

In proceedings of the Crime Victim Compensation Commission, the physician-patient privilege, the psychologist-patient privilege, the school counselor privilege, the social worker privilege, the counselor privilege and the husband-wife privilege do not apply to communications or records about the physical, mental or emotional condition of the claimant or victim if that condition is relevant to a claim for compensation.

In proceedings of the Crime Victim Compensation Commission, all medical information about the mental, physical, or emotional condition of a victim or claimant and all law enforcement records and information and any juvenile records are to be kept confidential by the Commission and its director. Except for this confidential information, the records of the Division are open to public inspection.

Crime Victim Compensation - Contested Case Hearings - N.C. Gen. Stat. § 15B-12

In contested case hearings on crime victim compensation, administrative law judges may request reports and information from law enforcement agencies and other State agencies. Information obtained in this manner is subject to the same privilege against public disclosure that may be asserted by the providing source.

Administrative law judges may have access to records of juvenile proceedings, which bear on the application for compensation. To the extent possible, administrative law judges are required to maintain the confidentiality of those records.

Administrative law judges may exclude all people from a hearing, except those involved in the hearing, while medical information and law enforcement investigative are being taken as evidence.

Except for information held confidential by administrative law judges, the official records of contested cases for crime victim compensation are open to public inspection.

Alcoholic Beverage Election Petitions - N.C. Gen. Stat. § 18B-601

County alcoholic beverage elections may be called by a petition, signed by at least 35% of the county's registered voters, filed with the county board of elections.

In a 1948 opinion, the North Carolina Attorney General said that once a petition is filed it becomes a public record, and the chairman of the county board of elections must permit it to be examined. 29 N.C.A.G. 697.

Social Security Numbers Used for Drivers License Administration - N.C. Gen. Stat. § 20-7(b1)

Drivers license applicants must give their social security numbers to the Division of Motor Vehicles in order to get their licenses. The Division may only use Social Security numbers for administering drivers license laws. Social Security numbers in the hands of the Division are not public records, and may not be disclosed. Violation of these disclosure restrictions is punishable under federal law.

Certificates of Disability Affecting Ability to Operate Motor Vehicles - N.C. Gen. Stat. § 20-7(e)

The Division of Motor Vehicles may require a drivers license applicant to submit medical certification regarding a physical defect or disease, which affects the applicant's operation of a motor vehicle. This certificate is confidential.

Division of Motor Vehicles - Records Collected in Drivers License Denial Proceedings - N.C. Gen. Stat. § 20-9(g)(4)h)

All records and evidence collected and compiled by the Division of Motor Vehicles and its reviewing board in proceedings concerning the denial of drivers licenses are not public records, and may be made available to the public only upon a court order.

Revocation of Drivers License for Incompetence, Alcoholism or Drug Addiction - N.C. Gen. Stat. § 20-17.1

Institutions where people have been committed involuntarily for treatment of alcoholism or drug addiction may be required to furnish information to the Division of Motor Vehicles for a determination as to whether the drivers licenses of people who are committed should be revoked. This information furnished to the Division is confidential.

Records Relating to Drivers Licenses - N.C. Gen. Stat. §§ 20-26(a) and (c), 20-27

The Division of Motor Vehicles keeps records of drivers license applications, tests, renewals, cancellations, revocations, disqualifications, and convictions and prayers for judgment that could lead to license revocation. All these records, except confidential medical reports for the current or previous five years are open to public inspection at any reasonable time during office hours, and copies are to be provided upon payment of fees as indicated in N.C. Gen. Stat. § 20-26.

Division of Motor Vehicles Records Open to Public Inspection - N.C. Gen. Stat. § 20-43

All records of the Division of Motor Vehicles, other than those declared by law to be confidential for the use of the Division, shall be open to public inspection during office hours.

Social Security Numbers in Automobile Registration - N.C. Gen. Stat. § 20-52

Motor vehicle owners must give their social security numbers to the Division of Motor Vehicles in order to get titles, registration cards and license plates. The Division may only use social security numbers for administering motor vehicle registrations laws. Social security numbers in the hands of the Division are not public records, and may not be disclosed. Violation of these disclosure restrictions is punishable under federal law.

Confidential File of Motor Vehicle Registrations for Public Law Enforcement Officials Whose Safety is at Risk - N.C. Gen. Stat. § 20-56

The Division of Motor Vehicles keeps a separate registration file for vehicles with private tags owned or leased by certain law enforcement personnel, Internal Revenue Service agents, and public officials whose personal safety would be risked if their registrations were subject to public disclosure. This separate registration file is confidential for the use of the Division.

Index of Regular License Plates on Highway Patrol Vehicles - N.C. Gen. Stat. § 20-84

Every year the Division of Motor Vehicles issues regular license plates in numerical sequence for use on Division vehicles assigned to the State Highway Patrol. An index of assignments of these plates is kept at Highway Patrol radio stations and the Division's registration division. Information as to the individual assignments of these plates is available to the public upon request to the same extent and in the same manner as regular registration information.

Motor Vehicle Collision Reports - N.C. Gen. Stat. § 20-166.1

When motor vehicles are involved in collisions involving injury, death or property damage over $500, or when operated vehicles are involved in collisions with parked or unattended vehicles, certain reports must be filed with law enforcement departments and the Division of Motor Vehicles. Law enforcement personnel and medical examiners are also required to file certain reports with the Division.

Collision reports filed with the Division by State, city or county police and medical examiners, but not other reports required under this section, are subject to public inspection at reasonable times.

In a 1988 opinion the North Carolina Attorney General said that law enforcement officers must forward collision investigation reports involving juveniles to the Division of Motor Vehicles, pursuant to N.C. Gen. Stat. § 20-166.1(e). Collision reports, in and of themselves, do not contain allegations of criminal offenses by juveniles. 58 N.C.A.G. 33 (1988).

Financing Statements for Secured Transactions - N.C. Gen. Stat. § 25-9-403

In order to perfect a security interest, a financing statement must be filed with a register of deeds and/or the Secretary of State's Office (depending on the type of collateral). The filing officer keeps all filed financing statements and must make them available for public inspection.

Depository for Wills - N.C. Gen. Stat. § 31-11

Superior court clerks have depositories in which people may file their wills for safekeeping. The contents of wills in the depository are not open to the inspection of anyone except the testator or an authorized representative until the will is offered for probate.

Multidisciplinary Evaluations in Incompetency Proceedings - N.C. Gen. Stat. § 35A-1111

To assist in determining the nature and extent of a person's disability, or to assist in developing a guardianship plan, in incompetency proceedings the clerk of court may order a multidisciplinary evaluation of the respondent. The evaluation is not a public record and its contents are to be released only as directed by the clerk.

Settlements in Housing Discrimination Cases - N.C. Gen. Stat. § 41A-7(d) and (g)(2)

The North Carolina Human Relations Commission resolves housing discrimination complaints. Nothing said or done in the course of the informal settlement procedure may be made public by the Commission or used as evidence in a later legal action under the State Fair Housing Act without the written consent of the person concerned.

A written conciliation agreement between the parties to a housing discrimination complaint must be made public unless the parties otherwise agree and the Commission determines that disclosure is not required to further the purposes of the State Fair Housing Act.

Land Plats - N.C. Gen. Stat. § 47-30(b)

All land plats registered with the registers of deeds must be in a clear format so that the public may get legible copies.

Pre-Adoption Reports - N.C. Gen. Stat. § 48-16(c)

When a petition for adoption is filed, the county director of social services conducts an investigation and makes a written report to the court on the suitability of the proposed adoption. These reports are not open to public inspection except upon order of the court.

Adoption Records - N.C. Gen. Stat. §§ 48-24, 48-25, and 48-26

The final order for an adoption is recorded in the public files of the office of the clerk of court. All other files on adoption proceedings are kept in the office of the clerk of court and at the North Carolina Department of Human Resources. None of these other files is open for general public inspection. It is a crime for people in charge of these files to disclose information contained in them.

Certain information about an adoptee's biological parents, other than information that would identify them, is provided to the county department of social services or licensed child placing agency. This information is available to adoptees, upon request, when they reach age 21. This information, if known, may include only 1) the adoptee's birth date and weight; 2) the age of the adoptee's biological parents (in years); 3) the nationality, ethnic background and race of the adoptee's biological parents; 4) the number of years of school completed by the adoptee's biological parents at the time of birth; and 5) the physical appearance of the biological parents at the adoptee's time of birth in terms of height, weight, color of hair, eyes and skin.

Adoption records may be opened by a judge, after a special private hearing, if disclosure is in the best interest of the child or of the public.

In *Sheppard v. Sheppard*, 38 N.C. App. 712, 248 S.E.2d 871 (1978), a woman suing for custody of her children subpoenaed the files of her former attorney, who had assisted her and her husband in adopting one of the children. The files contained information from the adoption case. The North Carolina Court of Appeals ruled that these documents were not admissible in the custody case because the woman had not obtained the documents in a proceeding under N.C. Gen. Stat. § 48-26, which is designed to ensure that adoption records are released only when appropriate.

Child Custody and Visitation Mediation - N.C. Gen. Stat. 50-13.1

In contested proceedings involving the custody or visitation of minor children, the court may order that contested issues be resolved in mediation. Mediation proceedings are held in private and are confidential. All verbal and written communications in a mediation proceeding are absolutely privileged and inadmissible in court.

Banking and Financial

Annual Report on Bank Takeovers by State Banking Commission - N.C. Gen. Stat. § 53-20(s)

The State Banking Commission may take possession of banks in certain circumstances. The Commissioner of Banks makes an annual report showing the condition of banks taken over by the Commission. This report is available for public inspection.

Change in Control of Banks - N.C. Gen. Stat. § 53-42.1

Before a person acquires voting stock of any bank or bank holding company that would result in a change in the control of the bank or holding company, the person must apply to the Commissioner of Banks for approval of the proposed acquisition. All of the information in an application or report filed for approval of stock acquisition, and all information produced by an investigation or examination of these reports or applications, is confidential and not available for public inspection.

Official Records of Commissioner of Banks - N.C. Gen. Stat. § 53-99

The Commissioner of Banks is required to keep a record in his office of his official acts, rulings and transactions. Much of this record is open to inspection, examination and copying by any person. However, there are 13 categories of records that are confidential and not subject to inspection. These confidential records include much of the information obtained in audits and investigations conducted by the Commissioner, and they include complaints from the public about banks. For a complete list of confidential records, consult the statute.

Bank Examiners Subject to Prosecution for Revealing Confidential Information - N.C. Gen. Stat. § 53-125

It is a crime for bank examiners and other employees of the Commissioner of Banks to disclose the facts and information obtained in bank examinations, except when legally required to report or act upon the information.

Appeal of Decisions of Commissioner of Banks - N.C. Gen. Stat. §§ 53-231, 53-232.17, 53-240, 53-252 and 53-272

Decisions of the Commissioner of Banks under the following laws may be appealed to the North Carolina Court of Appeals:

(1) the North Carolina Bank Holding Company Act of 1984 (N.C. Gen. Stat. § 53-231);

(2) the North Carolina International Bank Act (N.C. Gen. Stat. § 53-232.17);

(3) the Registration Requirements Act for Certain Makers of Mortgages and Deeds of Trust on Residential Real Property (N.C. Gen. Stat. § 53-240);

(4) the Refund Anticipation Loan Act (N.C. Gen. Stat. § 53-252); and

(5) the Reverse Mortgage Act (N.C. Gen. Stat. § 53-272).

The Commissioner must certify a record of the case to the Court. In appeals under all of these laws, the record includes factual information from Commission investigations and examinations, except that the Commissioner may exclude information he deems confidential. In all but the Reverse Mortgage Act, the Commissioner may exclude from the record trade secrets for which a party has made a claim of confidentiality.

Financial Privacy Act - N.C. Gen. Stat. § 53B

The Financial Privacy Act says that financial records at financial institutions are confidential, and financial institutions should not release financial records to government authorities except under certain circumstances, which are described in the statute.

In a 1989 opinion the North Carolina Attorney General said that the Financial Privacy Act applied to customers who open accounts at financial institutions using fictitious names. This is true even if the financial institution is the victim of an alleged crime by the customer. 59 N.C.A.G. 4 (1989).

Credit Union Division Records - N.C. Gen. Stat. § 54-109.105

The Credit Union Division in the Department of Commerce regulates and investigates credit unions. The following records of the Division are confidential and may not be disclosed:

(1) Information obtained or compiled in examinations, audits, and investigations of credit unions;

(2) Information reflecting collateral of named borrowers or specific withdrawable accounts of named members;

(3) Information in federal agency investigations and audits, if the information is confidential under federal law or regulations;

(4) Information and reports submitted by credit unions to federal regulatory agencies, if confidential under federal law or regulations;

(5) Complaints from credit union members received by the Division; and

(6) All records that would disclose any of this confidential information.

It is a criminal offense to make an unauthorized disclosure of this information. Employees who disclose this confidential information are liable to any person injured by the disclosure.

A court may order disclosure of specific information.

The private business and affairs of an individual or company may not be disclosed by Division employees or others who get this information in an authorized manner.

Information contained in an application for a new credit union is public information.

Savings Bank and Savings and Loan Association Records in the Savings Institutions Division - N.C. Gen. Stat. §§ 54B-63, 54B-66, 54C-60 and 54C-79

The Savings Institutions Commission and the Administrator of the Savings Institutions Division of the Department of Commerce regulate and investigate savings banks and savings and loan associations. The following records of the Commission and its agents are confidential and may not be disclosed:

(1) Information obtained or compiled in examinations, audits, and investigations of associations;

(2) Information reflecting collateral of named borrowers, amount of stock owned by named stockholders, savings bank stockholder lists required to be submitted by the Administrator, or specific withdrawable accounts of named members or customers;

(3) Information in federal agency investigations and audits, if the information is confidential under federal law or regulations;

(4) Information and reports submitted by associations to federal regulatory agencies, if confidential under federal law or regulations;

(5) Complaints and related material about associations from the public;

(6) All records that would disclose any of this confidential information.

The private business and affairs of an individual or company may not be disclosed by Savings Institution Division employees, Commission members, or others who get this information in an authorized manner.

It is a criminal offense to make an unauthorized disclosure of confidential information. Employees who disclose confidential information are liable to any person injured by the disclosure.

A court may order disclosure of specific information.

Information contained in an application is public information. However, disclosure does not extend to the financial information of the incorporators or to any further information deemed by the Administrator to be confidential.

Business Corporations - N.C. Gen. Stat. §§ 55-1-22(c) (Official Comment, Paragraph 2), 55-2-01, 55-5-01, 55-10-06, 55-11-05, 55-14-03, 55-15-03, and 55-16-22

Any person who wants a certified copy of a document filed with the Secretary of State under the North Carolina Business Corporation Act may get a copy by paying a prescribed fee.

Many corporate documents are required to, or may, be filed with the Secretary of State. These documents are available to the public. Among these documents are articles of incorporation, amendments to articles of incorporation, articles of dissolution, articles of merger or share exchange, authorizations for foreign corporations to transact business in North Carolina, registered offices and agents, and annual reports.

Corporations are required to file annual reports containing the corporation's name, state or country of incorporation, registered office and principal office, principal officers, directors, and a brief description of the nature of the corporation's business.

Secretary of State Interrogatories to Corporations and Companies - N.C. Gen. Stat. §§ 55-1-33, 55A-1-33, and 57C-1-33

The Secretary of State sends interrogatories (written questions requiring written answers) to business corporations, nonprofit corporations, and limited liability companies to determine their compliance with the corporation laws. Neither these interrogatories nor the answers to them are open to public inspection, and the Secretary of State may not disclose any information from them except as required by his official duties or as required as evidence in legal proceedings.

Insurance

Insurance - Rate Lists - N.C. Gen. Stat. § 58-2-40

The Commissioner of Insurance is required to compile lists of insurance rates, and to make those lists available to the public.

Insurance - Commissioner Records; Arson, Public Burning and Fraud Records - N.C. Gen. Stat. § 58-2-100

The office of the Commissioner of Insurance is a public office and the records, reports, books and papers there are available for public inspection. However, records compiled in investigations for arson, public burning and fraud are not public records and may be made available to the public only with a court order. A district attorney may obtain these files for crimes and investigations in his district.

Insurance - Patient Medical Records - N.C. Gen. Stat. § 58-2-105

Privileged patient medical records in the possession of the Department of

Insurance are not public records.

Insurance - Records of Examinations - N.C. Gen. Stat. §§ 58-2-131(l) and 58-2-132(d), (e), and (f)

Records of examinations of insurers may not be made public by the Commissioner of Insurance pending, during and after examinations until the insurer has either accepted or approved the final examination report or has been given an opportunity for an informal hearing to answer or rebut the report. Any informal hearing is private.

Once an examination report is finalized it is a public document open to public inspection, unless a court prevents its publication.

Insurance - License Revocations - N.C. Gen. Stat. § 58-2-133(c)

The Commissioner of Insurance may refuse, revoke or suspend the license of any insurer who refuses to submit to an examination or who refuses to pay examination fees. The Commissioner may publicize any of these license refusals, revocations or suspensions and may give the reasons for them.

Insurance - Professional Liability Insurance Annual Statements - N.C. Gen. Stat. § 58-2-170(a)

Insurers or others who provide professional liability insurance are required to submit annual statements concerning claims. These annual statements may not be reported or disclosed to the public in a way, which identifies individual health care providers or medical centers.

Insurance - Regulatory Information System Information - N.C. Gen. Stat. §§ 58-2-220 and 58-4-25

Financial test ratios, data or information generated by the Commissioner of Insurance pursuant to the NAIC Insurance Regulatory Information System or any similar or successor programs are not public records. This information is to be disseminated by the Commissioner consistent with procedures established by the NAIC.

Insurance - Employers Self-Insured for Workers' Compensation - N.C. Gen. Stat. § 58-2-230

The Commissioner of Insurance provides annually to the Department of Labor the names and addresses of employers who are self-insured for workers' compensation. This information is confidential and is not open for public inspection.

Insurance - Risk-Based Capital Reports & Plans; Corrective Orders - N.C. Gen. Stat. § 58-12-35

Risk-based capital plans, and risk-based capital reports (to the extent the information is not required to be made public in annual statement schedules) filed with the Commissioner of Insurance by insurers are to be kept confidential by the Commissioner, other than their publication for the purposes of enforcement actions by the Commissioner.

Insurance - Acquiring Control of Insurers - N.C. Gen. Stat. § 58-19-15

Before anyone acquires control of an insurer through stock transactions, mergers or other acquisitions, they must submit a statement to the Commissioner of Insurance and get approval for the acquisition. This statement must identify the source of any consideration used for the acquisition. If the source of that consideration is a loan made in the lender's ordinary course of business, the identity of the lender will remain confidential if the person filing the statement requests confidentiality.

Insurance - Insurance Holding Companies - N.C. Gen. Stat. § 58-19-40

Licensed insurers who are members of insurance holding companies must register with the Commissioner of Insurance and are required to submit certain information. The Commissioner may conduct examinations of these companies. All information reported to the Commissioner under these provisions is confidential and may not be made public without the written consent of the insurer. However, the Commissioner may publish any or all of this information if he determines that the interests of the insurer's policyholders or the public will be served by publication. Before publishing any of this information, the Commissioner must give these insurers, their affiliates, or acquiring parties an opportunity to be heard.

Insurance - Surplus Lines Insurance Licensees' Affidavits and Reports - N.C. Gen. Stat. §§ 58-21-35 and 58-21-80

Surplus lines insurance licensees are required to file written reports and affidavits with the Commissioner of Insurance within 30 days after placing any surplus lines insurance. These reports and affidavits identify the insured and the insurer, and they contain other information about the insurance. Licensees are also required to file with the Commissioner quarterly reports containing certain information about their surplus lines insurance transactions during the preceding quarter. These affidavits and reports are not public records.

Insurance - Records and Proceedings of Insurers Under Administrative Supervision - N.C. Gen. Stat. § 58-30-62

Insurers whose financial condition becomes impaired may come under the administrative supervision of the Commissioner of Insurance. All proceedings, hearings, notices, correspondence, reports, records and other information on administrative supervision are confidential. The Commissioner may make these proceedings or records public if he considers that it is in the best interests of the insurer, its insureds or creditors, or the general public.

These confidentiality provisions do not apply to hearings and records obtained upon the appointment of a receiver for the insurer by a court.

Insurance - Commissioner Proceedings and Judicial Reviews Related to Administrative Supervision of Insurers - N.C. Gen. Stat. § 58-30-70

Commissioner of Insurance proceedings on administrative supervision of insurers, judicial reviews of these proceedings, and all records of related to these proceedings are confidential unless the court orders or the insurer requests that they be made public.

Insurance - Payroll Deduction Insurance Proposals - N.C. Gen. Stat. § 58-31-60(c1)

An employee insurance committee reviews proposals submitted by insurers for payroll deduction insurance for State employees. The proposals are sealed when submitted to the committee. The committee opens all proposals in public and records them in the minutes of the committee. The proposals then become public records open to public inspection.

Insurance - Public Officers and Employees Liability Insurance Commission - N.C. Gen. Stat. § 58-32-10

The Public Officers and Employees Liability Insurance Commission acquires and oversees professional liability insurance coverage for public officers. In doing so, the Commission may get information regarding loss ratios, loss factors, loss experience and other data from any agency or company issuing professional liability insurance for public officers. The names of companies providing this information are not public records. However, the Commission may make the rest of this information public to show aggregate statistics for the State as a whole.

Insurance - Filings of North Carolina Rate Bureau - N.C. Gen. Stat. § 58-36-15

The North Carolina Rate Bureau files with the Commissioner of Insurance copies of the rates, classification plans, rating plans and rating system used by its members. These filings are open to public inspection immediately upon submission to the Commissioner.

Insurance - Experience Rate Modifier Information Provided to Department of Labor by North Carolina Rate Bureau - N.C. Gen. Stat. § 58-36-16

The North Carolina Rate Bureau provides information to the Department of Labor indicating each employer's experience rate modifier established for the purpose of setting premium rates for workers' compensation insurance and the name and business address of each employer whose workers' compensation coverage is provided through the assigned-risk pool. This information is confidential and not open for public inspection.

Insurance - Deviations from Established Rates - N.C. Gen. Stat. § 58-36-30

An insurer may charge a rate for insurance in excess of the rates established by the North Carolina Rate Bureau with the approval of the Commissioner of Insurance and the written consent of the insured. All data filed with the Commissioner applying for approval to charge higher rates are proprietary and confidential and are not public records.

Insurance Information and Privacy Act - N.C. Gen. Stat. § 58, Article 39

Insurance companies, agents and support organizations are restricted in how and to whom they may disclose personal and privileged information about individuals collected or received in connection with insurance transactions. The people and organizations that may receive this information, and the circumstances in which they may receive it, are listed at N.C. Gen. Stat. § 58-39-75.

Insurance - Rate Filings - N.C. Gen. Stat. § 58-40-35

Insurers are required to file with the Commissioner of Insurance rates and amendments and changes to rates, along with supporting data required by the Commissioner. All of this information, as soon as it is filed, is open to public inspection at any reasonable time. Any person may get copies upon request and payment of a reasonable charge.

Insurance - North Carolina Health Care Excess Liability Fund - N.C. Gen. Stat. §§ 58-47-15(d) and 58-47-50

Records held by the North Carolina Health Care Excess Liability Fund are not public records. However, the Board of Governors of the fund makes an annual report to the General Assembly and Governor. All these reports must be made available to the public.

Insurance - Postassessment Insurance Guaranty Association - N.C. Gen. Stat. § 58-48-60

The Board of Governors of the Post-assessment Insurance Guaranty Association may request that the Commissioner of Insurance conduct an examination of any member insurer whose financial condition may be hazardous to the policyholders or the public. The Board's request for an examination is kept on file by the Commissioner, but it is not open to public inspection prior to the release of the Commissioner's examination report to the public. As with other insurance examinations, the final report of the Commissioner's examination is made public.

The Board may also make reports and recommendations to the Commissioner on matters related to the solvency, liquidation, rehabilitation or conservation or any member insurer. These reports and recommendations are not public documents.

Insurance - Books and Records of Third Party Administrators - N.C. Gen. Stat. § 58-56-16

Third party administrators are required to keep complete books and records of all transactions performed on behalf of insurers. The Commissioner of Insurance has access to these books and records for the purposes of examinations, audits and inspections. The Commissioner must keep confidential any trace secrets contained in these books and records, including the identity and addresses of policyholders and certificate holders, except the Commissioner may use the information in judicial or administrative proceedings against third party administrators.

Insurance - Application for License as Third Party Administrator - N.C. Gen. Stat. § 58-56-51

Applicants for licenses as third party administrators must submit certain information about their businesses to the Commissioner of Insurance. This information, including any trade secrets, must be kept confidential, except the Commissioner may use the information in judicial or administrative proceedings against third party administrators.

Insurance - Annual Actuary Reports for Life Insurance Companies - N.C. Gen. Stat. § 58-58-50(j)(10)

Life insurance companies are required to submit to the Commissioner of Insurance an annual opinion from an actuary on the reserves and related actuarial items held in support of certain policies and contracts specified by the Commissioner. Materials submitted in support of these opinions must be kept confidential by the Commissioner and may not be made public.

However, this information may be released with the written consent of the company. It may also be released to the American Academy of Actuaries for disciplinary proceedings. None of the information remains confidential if any portion of it is released by another government agency other than a state insurance agency, or if it is released to the media or used in marketing by the company.

Insurance - Life and Health Insurance Guaranty Association Requests for Examinations of Delinquent Insurers - N.C. Gen. Stat. § 58-62-56(e)

The Board of Governors of the North Carolina Life and Health Insurance

Guaranty Association may request that the Commissioner of Insurance conduct an examination of any member insurer who may be delinquent. The Board's request for an examination is kept on file by the Commissioner, but it is not open to public inspection before the Commissioner releases the examination report to the public. The examination report may not be released to the Board before it is released to the public. As with other insurance examinations, the final report of the Commissioner's examination is made public.

Insurance - Records of Negotiations and Meetings with the Life and Health Insurance Guaranty Association - N.C. Gen. Stat. § 58-62-61(b)

Records are kept of all negotiations in which the North Carolina Life and Health Insurance Guaranty Association is involved in carrying out its duties. These records are made public only upon the termination of a liquidation, rehabilitation, or conservation proceeding involving a delinquent insurer, or upon a court order.

Insurance - Investigations of Continuing Care Facilities - N.C. Gen. Stat. § 58-64-50

The Commissioner of Insurance licenses and regulates continuing care facilities. In doing so, the Commissioner conducts investigations. These investigations may be public or private.

Insurance - Health Maintenance Organizations - N.C. Gen. Stat. §§ 58-67-175 and 58-67-180

All applications, filings and reports required under the Health Maintenance Organizations Act are public documents. However, information about the diagnosis, treatment, or health of any enrollee or applicant is confidential and may not be disclosed except as necessary to carry out the purposes of the Health Maintenance Organizations Act.

Insurance - Bail Bondsmen and Runners - N.C. Gen. Stat. §§ 58-71-115 and 58-71-125

Insurers who terminate the appointment of a surety bondsman are required to file a notice with the Commissioner of Insurance stating the reasons for the termination. Bail bondsmen who terminate the appointment of a runner must do the same. The information furnished in these notices is privileged and may not be used as evidence in any actions against the insurers or the bail bondsmen, respectively.

Insurance - State Fire and Rescue Commission - N.C. Gen. Stat. § 58-78-10(c)

All meetings of the State Fire and Rescue Commission are open to the public.

Insurance - Attorney General Fire Investigation Reports - N.C. Gen. Stat. § 58-79-1

The Attorney General, through the State Bureau of Investigation and in conjunction with local fire and law enforcement departments, investigates all fires in the State to determine whether they were caused by carelessness or design. A record of all these fire investigation reports is kept in the Attorney General's Office. The reports are open to public inspection at all times.

Utilities

Utilities Commission Records of Activities - N.C. Gen. Stat. § 62-19

The Utilities Commission is required to keep a record of ts official acts, rulings, orders, decisions and transactions and a current calendar of its scheduled activities and hearings. These documents are public records.

Utilities Commission Accident/Incident Investigation Reports - N.C. Gen. Stat. § 62-41

The Utilities Commission investigates accidents on public railroads or highways involving public utilities and incidents involving natural gas pipelines. Information obtained in these investigations must be written in a report and filed in the Commission office. These reports are subject to public inspection.

Natural Gas Pipeline Accident Reports - N.C. Gen. Stat. §62-50(a)

The Utilities Commission inspects and investigates natural gas pipeline facilities. Any information obtained during an investigation by the Commission of a natural gas accident or incident is put in writing and filed with the Commission clerk. These reports are subject to public inspection, but they are not admissible as evidence in any criminal or civil proceeding resulting from the incident.

Utilities Commission Hearings - N.C. Gen. Stat. § 62-71

All hearings of the Utilities Commission, Commission panels, individual commissioners, and examiners are public. Full records of hearings must be kept. Parties to proceedings are entitled to copies of records upon payment of reasonable costs.

Proposed Changes in Public Utility Rates - N.C. Gen. Stat. § 62-134(a)

Before public utilities may change their rates, they must file proposed changes with the Utilities Commission. These proposed changes are open for public inspection.

Utility Rates, Service Regulations, and Service Contracts - N.C. Gen. Stat. § 62-138

Public utilities are required to file all schedules of rates, service regulations, and forms of service contracts with the Utilities Commission. These utilities are required to keep these items open to public inspection. However, the Commission may waive public disclosure of rates if disclosure would cause the utility to suffer a competitive disadvantage.

All regular route common carriers of commodities and passengers, and all irregular route common carriers must file rate schedules with the Utilities Commission, and they must keep those schedules open for public inspection.

Electric membership corporations must file all rates, rate schedules, charges, service regulations, and forms of service contracts with the Utilities Commission, and they must keep these items open for public inspection.

Proposed Changes for Bus Company Rates - N.C. Gen. Stat. § 62-146.1(d)

Before bus companies, which provide fixed route service, may change their rates, they must file proposed changes with the Utilities Commission. These proposed changes are open for public inspection.

Motor Contract Carrier Rates - N.C. Gen. Stat. § 62-147

Motor contract carriers must file with the Utilities Commission, publish, and keep open for public inspection schedules of minimum rates for intrastate property transportation and any rules, regulations or practices affecting these rates.

Customer Information Submitted to 911 Emergency Telephone Systems - N.C. Gen. Stat. § 62A-9

Local governments may require telephone companies to submit customer telephone numbers, names, and service addresses to 911 emergency telephone systems. Local governments may not release the telephone numbers required to be provided by this section to anyone for purposes other than including the number in the emergency telephone system database or providing emergency services.

Scrap Purchasers - N.C. Gen. Stat. § 66-10

Purchasers of certain scrap and surplus materials, including rubber, leather, glass, waste paper, burlap cloth, cordage, and belting scrap are required to keep registers with certain information about these purchases. These registers are open to public inspection at all times. Failure to comply with this requirement is a criminal offense.

Lists of Partners in Professional Partnerships - N.C. Gen. Stat. § 66-68

In counties where they do business under an assumed name, businesses are required to file certain information about themselves with county registers of deeds. Instead of making separate filings in several counties, partnerships providing professional services may file this information annually with their professional licensing boards. These listings with professional licensing boards are open to public inspection during normal working hours.

Precious Metals Dealers - N.C. Gen. Stat. § 66-169

Precious metals dealers are required to keep record books containing information about the metals they purchase and the sellers they purchase them from. Dealers are required to file all new entries in these books with local law enforcement agencies within 48 hours after the underlying transaction. The files of local law enforcement agencies containing this information are not subject to public inspection. It is a crime for any public official or employee to provide access to these files.

Information on Archaeological Resources - N.C. Gen. Stat. § 70-18

Information about the nature and location of archaeological resources may be made available to the public under the public records law unless the Department of Cultural Resources determines that the disclosures would create a risk of harm to these resources or to the site at which these resources are located.

Mine Safety Advisory Council - N.C. Gen. Stat. § 74-24.6(b)

Meetings of the Mine Safety Advisory Council are open to the public.

Mine Accident Reports - N.C. Gen. Stat. § 74-24.13

Mine operators are required to submit to the Commissioner of Labor certain information about mine accidents, injuries and occupational diseases. The Commissioner compiles reports and findings based on the operators' reports. All these reports may be published by the Commissioner, and are available for public inspection.

Uranium Exploration Information - N.C. Gen. Stat. § 74-88

Companies and others engaged in uranium exploration are required to submit certain information to the Department of Labor. If these companies show to the Department's satisfaction that logs, survey plats and reports required to be filed with the Department are of a proprietary value related to their competitive rights, the information will be kept confidential and not subject to public inspection for four years after it is submitted to the Department. These confidentiality requests may be renewed and approved for two-year periods following the first four-year period.

Motor Fuel Prices - N.C. Gen. Stat. § 75-88

Motor fuel refiners or terminal suppliers who compute the prevailing prices under certain provisions of the Motor Fuel Marketing Act (N.C. Gen. Stat. § 75-81(4(a)(i) or (ii) are required to disclose the price publicly.

Watercraft Registration Records - N.C. Gen. Stat. § 75A-5(f)

Certain vessels must be registered with the Wildlife Resources Commission. The Commissioner collects and maintains information related to vessel registration. All these records are public records.

Local Water Safety Committee Meetings - N.C. Gen. Stat. § 75A-26(f)

All meetings of local water safety committees are open to the public. Where an existing organization or committee has received sponsorship, all its meetings devoted to carrying out the advisory functions of a local committee are open to the public.

Lake Wylie Marine Commission - N.C. Gen. Stat. § 77-34

The provisions of the open meetings law apply to meetings of the Lake Wylie Marine Commission that are held in North Carolina.

High Rock Lake Marine Commission - N.C. Gen. Stat. § 77-54

The provisions of the open meetings law apply to meetings of the High Rock Lake Marine Commission.

Securities Dealers and Salesmen Registration - N.C. Gen. Stat. § 78A-50

Securities dealers and salesmen are required to register with the Administrator of the North Carolina Securities Act (Secretary of State), and to submit certain information to the Administrator in doing so. The Administrator keeps a register of all applications for registration, registration statements, and all denial, suspension, or revocation orders. This register is open for public inspection.

The information contained in or filed with any registration statement, application, or report, may be made public by the Administrator under rules he prescribes.

The Administrator must furnish certified or regular copies of register entries or other public records upon payment of reasonable charges set by the Administrator.

Tender Offer Disclosures - N.C. Gen. Stat. § 78B-4(i)

People and companies who plan to make tender offers for equity securities must first submit certain information to the Administrator of the North Carolina Tender Offer

Disclosure Act (Secretary of State). All documents and materials filed with the Administrator are available for public inspection and copying. The Administrator must keep all these materials in his office for three years, and may destroy them after that.

Investment Advisors - N.C. Gen. Stat. §§ 78C-26(b), 78C-27(g), and 78C-31

Investment advisors must register with the Administrator of the North Carolina Investment Advisors Act (Secretary of State) and they must submit information to the Administrator.

The Administrator may make public or private investigations to determine compliance with the investment advisors law. The Administrator and his employees may not disclose any information not made public by the Administrator.

Hearings in administrative proceedings under this law are public unless the Administrator grants a request, joined in by all the respondents, that the hearing be private.

The Administrator keeps a register of all applications for registration, registration statements, and all denial, suspension, or revocation orders. This register is open for public inspection.

The information contained in or filed with any registration statement, application, or report may be made public by the Administrator under rules he prescribes.

The Administrator must furnish certified or regular copies of register entries or other public records upon payment of reasonable charges set by the Administrator.

Athlete Agents - N.C. Gen. Stat. § 78C-73

Athlete agents must register with and are subject to regulation by the Secretary of State. The Secretary may make public or private investigations of athlete agents to determine compliance with the athlete agents law. The Secretary may publish information on any violation of the athlete agents law or any rule or order under the law.

Commodities Trading - N.C. Gen. Stat. §§ 78D-21, 78D-25 and 78D-30

Commodities traders are subject to regulation by the Administrator of the North Carolina Commodities Act (Secretary of State). The Administrator may make public or private investigations to determine violations of the Commodities Act. The following is not public information:

(1) Information obtained in private investigations;

(2) Information that is confidential under the public records law; and

(3) Information obtained from federal agencies, which may not be disclosed under federal law.

All other information collected, assembled or kept by the Administrator under the Commodities Act is available for examination by the public.

Hearings in administrative proceedings under this law are public unless the Administrator grants a request, joined in by all the respondents, that the hearing be private.

Trademark Registration - N.C. Gen. Stat. § 80-7

The Secretary of State keeps for public examination all registered and assigned trademarks.

Licensed Professionals and Professional Boards

Attorney Licensing Records - N.C. Gen. Stat. § 84-24

Records containing information collected and compiled by the Board of Law Examiners from investigations, inquiries or interviews connected with attorney examinations or licensing matters are not public records.

North Carolina State Bar - N.C. Gen. Stat. § 84-33

Annual meetings of the North Carolina State Bar are open to members in good standing.

Record of Registered Barbers and Apprentices - N.C. Gen. Stat. § 86A-21

The State Board of Barber Examiners keeps a record of actions regarding the licenses of registered barbers and barbers' apprentices. This record is open to public inspection at all reasonable times.

Roster of Licensed Contractors - N.C. Gen. Stat. § 87-8

The secretary of the State Licensing Board for General Contractors prepares an annual roster of licensed contractors. This roster is available to the public at cost, or at no cost as directed by the Board.

Records of Plumbing, Heating, and Fire Sprinkler Contractors Board - N.C. Gen. Stat. § 87-20

The State Board of Examiners of Plumbing, Heating and Fire Sprinkler Contractors keeps records of its proceedings and a register of all applicants for examination.

In a 1951 opinion the North Carolina Attorney General said these records are public records, and certified copies must be given to people who request them. 31 N.C.A.G. 82 (1951)

Registry of Licensed Electrical Contractors - N.C. Gen. Stat. § 87-43

The State Board of Examiners of Electrical Contractors keeps a registry of licensed electrical contractors. This registry is open for public inspection during ordinary business hours.

Cosmetologist Records - N.C. Gen. Stat. § 88-29

The Board of Cosmetic Art Examiners keeps a record of its proceedings concerning certificates of registration for cosmetologists, including a list of all registered cosmetologists and apprentices. This record is open to public inspection everyday, except Sundays and legal holidays.

Board Investigations of Engineers and Surveyors - N.C. Gen. Stat. § 89C-10

The State Board of Registration for Engineers and Surveyors licenses and regulates engineers and surveyors. The Board may investigate registrants. Investigation information is confidential until the Board issues a citation to the registrant.

Landscape Contractor Register - N.C. Gen. Stat. § 89D-6

The secretary-treasurer of the North Carolina Landscape Contractors' Licensing Board keeps a current roster of registered titled landscape contractors in the Board's office. This register is open to public inspection.

Geologist Licensing Records - N.C. Gen. Stat. § 89E-14 and § 89E-15

The North Carolina Board for the Licensing of Geologists keeps a public record of its proceedings and a register of applicants. Except as required by law or rule, individual test scores, and applications and related materials (including references), are confidential.[27]

The Board also publishes annually a roster of licensed geologists. Copies of this roster are available to the public upon request and payment of a reasonable copying fee set by the Board.

In a 1991 opinion the North Carolina Attorney General confirmed the confidentiality of these materials. 60 N.C.A.G. 76 (1991)

Reports to Board of Medical Examiners Concerning Physician Privileges and Malpractice Insurance - N.C. Gen. Stat. § 90-14.13

Health care institutions are required to report revocations, suspensions, or limitations of physicians' privileges and physicians' resignations from practice to the North Carolina Board of Medical Examiners. Insurance companies are required to report to the Board damages or settlements against insured physicians, and cancellations and non-renewals of professional liability coverage of physicians for cause. These reports are privileged and not open to the public.

Physician Licensing and Disciplinary Records - N.C. Gen. Stat. § 90-16

The North Carolina Board of Medical Examiners is required to publish the names of newly licensed physicians in three daily North Carolina newspapers within 30 days after licenses are granted.

Records collected or compiled by the Board in licensing and disciplinary investigations are not public records. However, notices to licensees of charges or of hearings are public records, even if they contain information from investigations. Also, once investigation information is admitted into evidence in Board hearings, it becomes a public record.

When releasing investigation information as just described, the Board may withhold (from public disclosure) the identity of a patient who has not consented to public disclosure of treatment by the accused physician. Also, the Board may receive evidence in a closed session involving a patient who has not consented to disclosure of treatment by the accused physician.

In *In re Sullivan*, 112 N.C. App. 795, 436 S.E.2d 862 (1993), the North Carolina Court of Appeals held that the Board has some responsibility to ensure that records it keeps on licensees are accurate. A doctor who was the subject of disciplinary proceedings petitioned the Board to expunge certain information in his records that he claimed was false and prejudicial. The Board denied his request. The Court of Appeals held that the doctor's request was a "contested case" under the Administrative Procedure Act, and he was entitled to a hearing before the Board could deny his request. The Court also said that although N.C. Gen. Stat. § 90-16 does not specifically set forth guidelines for expunging information from its files, the statute carries with it a responsibility to assure that there is a factual basis for any records it keeps and to assure that records kept pursuant to the statute are accurate. The Court said this requirement is both reasonable and critically important when the records bear on one's license to engage in an occupational livelihood.

Patient Information Obtained in Physician and Physician Assistant Peer Reviews - N.C. Gen. Stat. § 90-21.22

The North Carolina Medical Society and its local medical society components, and the North Carolina Academy of Physician Assistants, conduct peer reviews of impaired physicians and physician assistants. These groups report information from these reviews to the North Carolina Board of Medical Examiners. Confidential patient information and other nonpublic information obtained or created in this process remains confidential and may not be obtained in civil cases.

Elections of Board of Dental Examiners - N.C. Gen. Stat. § 90-22(c)(12)

For the purpose of keeping track of balloting in elections for membership to the North Carolina Board of Dental Examiners, an official list of licensed dentists is kept at the office of North Carolina Board of Dental Elections and is open to the inspection of any person at all times. Copies may be made by any licensed dentist.

Dentist Licensing and Disciplinary Records - N.C. Gen. Stat. § 90-41(g)

The North Carolina State Board of Dental Examiners licenses and disciplines dentists. Records collected or compiled by the Board in licensing and disciplinary investigations are not public records. However, notices to licensees of charges or of hearings are public records, even if they contain information from investigations. Also, once investigation information is admitted into evidence in Board hearings, it becomes a public record.

Patient Information Obtained in Dentist Peer Reviews - N.C. Gen. Stat. §§ 90-48.2 and 90-48.10

Peer review organizations conduct peer reviews of impaired dentists. These organizations report information from these reviews to the North Carolina State Board of Dental Examiners. Confidential patient information and other nonpublic information obtained or created in this process remains confidential and may not be obtained in civil cases.

Also, the proceedings and records of a dental peer review committee (except those concerning the investigation and consideration of Medicare and Medicaid charges and payments) are to be held in confidence and may not be used as evidence. However, information that is available from other sources is not immune from use as evidence merely because it was presented during dental peer review proceedings.

Chiropractor Access to Laboratory Records - N.C. Gen. Stat. § 90-153

Licensed chiropractors have access to their patients' X-ray and laboratory records at publicly supported hospitals. This provision was confirmed in a 1978 opinion by the North Carolina Attorney General. 48 N.C.A.G. 32 (1978).

Meetings of North Carolina Medical Veterinary Board - N.C. Gen. Stat. § 90-183

The North Carolina Medical Veterinary Board holds at least four meetings a year. All meetings are open to the public, except that the Board may meet in closed session to prepare, approve, administer, or grade examinations, or to deliberate the qualification of an applicant for license or the disposition of a proceeding to discipline a veterinarian.

Board of Podiatry Examiners - List of Licensed Podiatrists - N.C. Gen. Stat. § 90-202.4(g)

The Board of Podiatry Examiners for the State of North Carolina keeps a list of the names and addresses of each licensed podiatrist in the State. This list is available for inspection.

North Carolina Board of Opticians - N.C. Gen. Stat. § 90-239

The North Carolina Board of Opticians meets at least once a year. The Board's secretary keeps a record of Board proceedings. This record is open to public inspection at all reasonable times.

Psychologist Licensing and Disciplinary Records - N.C. Gen. Stat. § 90-270.15

The North Carolina Psychology Board licenses and disciplines psychologists.

Records collected or compiled by the Board in licensing and disciplinary investigations are not public records. However, notices to licensees of charges or of hearings are public records, even if they contain information from investigations. Also, once investigation information is admitted into evidence in Board hearings, it becomes a public record.

When investigation information is released or admitted as evidence as just described, the Board may delete information about the identity of a patient who has not consented to public disclosure of treatment by the accused psychologist. Also, the Board may receive evidence in a closed session involving a patient who has not consented to disclosure of treatment by the accused psychologist.

Fee-Based Practicing Pastoral Counselors - N.C. Gen. Stat. § 90-390

The North Carolina State Board of Examiners of Fee-Based Practicing Pastoral Counselors certifies and disciplines fee-based pastoral counselors and associates.

In records involving discipline or refusals by the Board to certify counselors, the Board must try to withhold, from public disclosure, the identity of any clients who have not consented to disclosure of their treatment by a counselor or associate.

Records collected or compiled by the Board in certification and disciplinary investigations are not public records. However, notices to licensees of charges or of hearings are public records, even if they contain information from investigations. Also, once investigation information is admitted into evidence in Board hearings, it becomes a public record.

When investigation information is released or admitted as evidence as just described, the Board may delete information about the identity of a client who has not consented to public disclosure of treatment by the accused counselor or associate. Also, the Board may receive evidence in a closed session involving a client who has not consented to disclosure of treatment by the accused counselor or associate.

State Board of Sanitarian Examiners - N.C. Gen. Stat. § 90A-59

The State Board of Sanitarian Examiners keeps the following records, all of which are public records:

(1)   Records of its proceedings;

(2)   A register of all applications for registration of sanitarians; and

(3)   A current registry of registered sanitarians and sanitarian interns.

North Carolina Real Estate Commission - N.C. Gen. Stat. §§ 93A-5 and 93A-53

The Executive Director of the North Carolina Real Estate Commission keeps a roster of licensed real estate brokers and real estate salesmen, and a roster of registered time-share projects. These rosters are open to public inspection.

Occupational Licensing Board Annual Reports - N.C. Gen. Stat. § 93B-2

Each occupational licensing board is required to file with the Secretary of State and the Attorney General an annual financial report, and an annual report containing the address of the board, the names of its members and officers, and various numerical data on licenses applied for, granted, suspended, or revoked. These reports are open to public inspection.

Occupational Licensing Boards - Registers of Licensees - N.C. Gen. Stat. §93B-3

Every occupational licensing board is required to keep a register of all people currently licensed by the board. Each year licensing boards update their registers with new licenses issued, licenses revoked or suspended, and licensees who have died. Licensing boards are required to provide the licensed status of any individual to any citizen of the State who requests it.

In a 1976 opinion the North Carolina Attorney General said that applications for licensure and other documentary licensing information received by the Board of Examiners for Speech and Language Pathologists and Audiologists are public records and are subject to public inspection. 45 N.C.A.G. 188 (1975).

North Carolina Hearing Aid Dealers and Fitters Board - N.C. Gen. Stat. § 93D-3(b)

The secretary and treasurer of the North Carolina Hearing Aid Dealers and Fitters Board keep a full record of the Board's proceedings and a current list of all licenses. These records are open to public inspection at all reasonable times.

North Carolina Appraisal Board - N.C. Gen. Stat. § 93E-1-11(b)

The executive director of the North Carolina Appraisal Board keeps, in the Board's office, a current roster of all State-licensed and State-certified real estate appraisers. This roster is open to public inspection.

Pharmacy Records - N.C. Gen. Stat. § 90-85.36

Written prescription orders on file in pharmacies or other places where prescriptions are dispensed are not public records. These orders may be released to 14 categories of people or organizations, who are listed in the statute. These people and organizations include certain patients, physicians, insurance companies and people related to patients. For a complete listing, consult the statute.

A pharmacist or his authorized agent may disclose any information, but only when necessary to protect a person's life or health.

Pharmacists are required to keep a list of people to whom they dispense certain types of drugs known as Schedule V substances (these substances are listed at N.C. Gen. Stat. § 90-93). This list of people is not a public record, but it may be disclosed at the pharmacist's discretion.

Expunction of Records Under the North Carolina Controlled Substances Act - N.C. Gen. Stat. §§ 90-96 and 90-113.14

The North Carolina Controlled Substances Act (Article 5, Chapter 90 of the General Statutes) defines several crimes involving the possession and use of certain drugs and drug paraphernalia. Certain first-time offenders under 21 who plead guilty or are found guilty to certain misdemeanors may apply to the court for discharge and dismissal of charges, conditioned on their participation in drug education programs. Other first-time offenders convicted of certain misdemeanors may apply to the court for cancellation of their convictions.

If courts grant these discharges or cancellations, they may order that court and law enforcement records of these defendants' arrests, indictments or information, trials, and convictions be expunged.

If records are expunged, the clerk of court sends a list of people whose records are expunged to the Administrative Office of the Courts, which keeps a file of these names. This file is confidential. Names in the file may be disclosed only to judges to determine if people charged with offenses were previously granted discharges or if their convictions were cancelled.

Controlled Substance Records - N.C. Gen. Stat. § 90-107

Prescriptions, order forms and records required to kept by the Controlled Substances Act, and stocks of controlled substances, are open for inspection only to federal and State officers enforcing controlled substances laws. Officers may not divulge this information to anyone else.

Records of Treatment for Drug Dependence - N.C. Gen. Stat. § 90-109.1

Under the North Carolina Controlled Substances Act, people may request treatment and rehabilitation from medical practitioners. These medical practitioners and their employees may not disclose the names of these patients to law enforcement personnel, and information about the patients may not be used in court unless authorized by the patient.

Medical practitioners who provide drug treatment and rehabilitation are required to submit periodic, nonidentifying statistics on those they treat to the North Carolina Department of Human Resources. The Department compiles periodic reports of these statistics. These Department reports are public records.

Department of Labor Investigation Records - N.C. Gen. Stat. §95-25.20

The Department of Labor enforces the Wage and Hour Act and the Retaliatory Employment Discrimination Act. Files and records of investigations and enforcement proceedings under these laws are not subject to inspection and examination under the public records law. Parties subject to these proceedings may get these records through civil discovery.

Private Personnel Service Advisory Council - N.C. Gen. Stat. § 95-47.7(c)

All meetings of the North Carolina Private Personnel Service Advisory council are open to the public, and all records of the Council are open to the public, except as otherwise prescribed by law.

Elevator Safety Act, Amusement Device Safety Act, and Occupational Safety and Health Act Records - N.C. Gen. Stat. §§ 95-110.14, 95-111.17 and 95-152

The Commissioner of Labor inspects and regulates elevators, amusement devices, and work places for safety and health. All information reported to or obtained by the Commissioner in investigations or proceedings under the Elevator Safety Act, the Amusement Device Safety Act, and the Occupational Safety and Health Act of North Carolina which might reveal a trade secret are confidential, except when it is used to carry out the Act or when it is relevant in proceedings. In these proceedings, the Commissioner or the court may issue orders to protect the confidentiality of trade secrets.

State Advisory Council on Occupational Safety and Health - N.C. Gen. Stat. § 95-134

The State Advisory Council on Occupational Safety and Health advises the Commissioner of Labor on occupational safety and health. The Council holds at least two meetings each year. All meetings are open to the public, and a transcript is kept and made available for public inspection.

Toxic Vapors Act - Conditional Discharge - N.C. Gen. Stat. § 90-113.14(c)

Certain people may be granted conditional discharges of their convictions under the Toxic Vapors Act. The Administrative Office of the Courts keeps a confidential file of people who are granted conditional discharges. The information in this file is made available only to judges to determine if people convicted under the Controlled Substances Act or the Toxic Vapors Act have been previously granted a conditional discharge.

Safety and Health Review Board - N.C. Gen. Stat. § 95-135(c)

The Safety and Health Review Board hears appeals from occupational safety and health citations and abatements. Every official act of the Board is entered of record, and the Board's hearings and records are open to the public.

Occupational Safety and Health Programs of State and Local Agencies - N.C. Gen. Stat. § 95-148

State agencies, local governments and other government subdivisions are required to have occupational safety and health programs. The Commissioner of Labor has access to records and reports kept and filed under these programs, unless the records are required to be kept secret in the interest of national defense. In those cases, the Commissioner may have access to other information that would not jeopardize national defense if released.

Hazardous Chemical Emergency Information to be Supplied to Fire Chiefs - N.C. Gen. Stat. § 95-194(e)

Employers who store certain amounts of hazardous chemicals at a facility are required to provide information about those chemicals to the fire chief who has jurisdiction over the facility. The fire chief may require the employer to prepare an emergency response plan for the facility. The fire chief is required to make this information available to personnel responsible for preplanning emergency response, police, medical or fire activities. However, the fire chief and others receiving this information may not otherwise distribute or disclose this information. Unauthorized disclosure of this information is a criminal offense.

This prohibition on further disclosure of this information does not apply to information that is available to the public as community information on hazardous chemicals. See, N.C. Gen. Stat. § 95-208.

Hazardous Substance Trade Secret Information - N.C. Gen. Stat. § 95-197

Employers are required to disclose to fire chiefs and to the public certain information about hazardous substances they produce, use or store (See, Community Information on Hazardous Chemicals - N.C. Gen. Stat. § 95-208 and Hazardous Chemical Emergency Information - N.C. Gen. Stat. § 95-194). An employer who believes all or part of the information required to be disclosed is a hazardous substance trade secret may withhold the information. However, the employer must still supply the information to the fire chief, who must hold it in confidence.

Members of the public may ask the Commissioner of Labor to review a claim that a hazardous substance is a trade secret. Any hearings held as a result of these requests are held in camera (in private). The Commissioner of Labor and the fire chief are required not to disclose this information. Unauthorized disclosure is a criminal offense.

Hazardous Chemical Emergency Information to be Supplied to Health Care Providers - N.C. Gen. Stat. § 95-198

A chemical manufacturer, importer or employer must provide the specific chemical identity of a hazardous chemical to a health care provider immediately if the provider determines it is necessary for emergency treatment, even if the information is a trade secret. The manufacturer, importer or employer may require a confidentiality agreement as soon as circumstances permit.

In nonemergency situations, the manufacturer, importer or employer may require a confidentiality agreement before treatment.

Community Information on Hazardous Chemicals - N.C. Gen. Stat. § 95-208

Any person in North Carolina may request certain information about hazardous chemicals in writing from employers who manufacture, process, use, store or produce hazardous chemicals. Employers are required to provide this information within 10 days. They may charge a fee not exceeding the cost of reproduction. If an employer refuses to provide the requested information, the person making the request may ask the

Commissioner of Labor to review the request. The Commissioner may require disclosure through legal proceedings.

Retaliatory Employment Actions - N.C. Gen. Stat. § 95-242

The Commissioner of Labor investigates, conciliates and seeks legal enforcement in cases of employment discrimination against people with sickle cell anemia, and cases of employer retaliation against employees who file complaints, testify, or otherwise exercise their rights under the North Carolina Workers' Compensation Act, the Occupational Safety and Health Act of North Carolina, and the Mine Safety and Health Act of North Carolina. Nothing said or done during informal conciliation procedures may be made public by the Commissioner or used as evidence in subsequent proceedings without the written consent of the people concerned.

The Commissioner's investigation and enforcement files and records are not subject to inspection and examination as public records while these investigations or enforcement proceedings are going on.

Employment Security Commission - N.C. Gen. Stat. §§ 96-4(c), (m) and (t), and 96-10(b)(2)

The Employment Security Commission of North Carolina administers the Employment Security Law (unemployment insurance and job service).

The Commission prints copies of the Employment Security Law, the Commission's regulations and rules, and other information it feels is relevant. Copies are available to the public upon application.

The Commission holds hearings to determine the rights of employers under the Employment Security Law. These hearings are open to the public.

Information obtained from employers and individuals in the administration of the Employment Security Law may not be disclosed except to the parties to a claim as necessary to enable them to present their claims and defenses. The Commission may also provide some of this information to other public officials and government agencies, as specified in the statute (For example, child support proceedings and State Controller).

Information obtained from employers, workers and applicants in the State Public Employment Service Program ("Job Service") may not be disclosed except as permitted to administer the program. The Employment Service Division publicizes information about job openings and applicants for the purpose of supplying the demand for workers and employment. The Labor Market Information Division is authorized to publish statistical information about work under the Commission's jurisdiction without revealing the identities of applicants or employers. The Commission may also provide some of this information to other government agencies, as specified in the statute.

Representatives of the Commission may examine county tax listings and other information required to be filed with county tax supervisors under the State's tax laws. The Commission may not make this information public.

It is a criminal offense for the Commissioner to disclose employment security information in an unauthorized manner.

North Carolina Industrial Commission - N.C. Gen. Stat. §§ 97-79(d), 97-81(b) and 97-92

Worker's compensation hearings before the North Carolina Industrial Commission, are open to the public. However, informal Commission hearings on an employer's notice of termination or suspension of workers compensation for an employee (N.C. Gen. Stat. § 97-18.1) are not open to the public.

Employers are required to file worker accident and injury reports with the Commission. These reports are private Commission records and are not open to public inspection. The parties involved in the accidents and injuries may inspect these reports.

The Commission publishes an annual statistical report on accident information received from employers. This annual report may not contain the names of employers and employees.

North Carolina Radiation Protection Act - N.C. Gen. Stat. §§ 104E-9(a)(4) and 104E-29

The Department of Environment, Health, and Natural Resources collects and disseminates information on the sources of radiation. The Department may refuse to publicize any of this information if disclosure is inconsistent with the stated policy of the Radiation Protection Act (found in N.C. Gen. Stat. § 104E-3) and disclosure would be against the health, welfare and safety of the public.

The Department monitors and regulates nuclear facilities. The following information received or prepared by the Department in carrying out its duties under the Radiation Protection Act is confidential information and not subject to disclosure:

(1) Trade secrets;

(2) Information that is confidential under federal or state law; and

(3) Information compiled in anticipation of enforcement or criminal proceedings, but only to the extent that disclosure would interfere with those proceedings.

It is a criminal offense to make unauthorized disclosure of this confidential information.

Southeast Interstate Low-Level Radioactive Waste Management Commission - N.C. Gen. Stat. § 104F-1, Article IV(d)

The Southeast Interstate Low-Level Radioactive Waste Management Commission meets at least once a year. Meetings are open to the public.

Controlled Substance Tax - N.C. Gen. Stat. § 105-113.112

Dealers of certain illegal drugs are required to pay an excise tax on the controlled substances they possess. Dealers are required to report to the Department of Revenue the amounts of tax due in accordance with a rate schedule in the statute. Information obtained pursuant to this law is confidential and may not be disclosed or used in a criminal prosecution. Unauthorized disclosure of this information is a criminal offense.

The Secretary of Revenue may publish statistics that do not disclose the identities of dealers or the contents of particular returns or reports.

Revenue Statistics - N.C. Gen. Stat. § 105-256

The Secretary of Revenue is required to prepare periodic reports on the collection and expenditure of certain taxes. The Secretary is also required to publish a taxpayer's bill of rights. The Secretary is required to deliver copies of these documents without charge to certain government agencies. The Secretary is required to distribute one copy of the taxpayer's bill of rights to taxpayers who are contacted by the Department of Revenue regarding the determination or collection of a tax (other than just providing a tax form), and upon request to other taxpayers.

Others may get copies of these reports upon payment of a fee that covers publication or copying costs and mailing costs.

Business Inventories Filed with County Tax Assessors - N.C. Gen. Stat. § 105-296(h)

County tax assessors may require all county residents and businesses to list taxable property. In a 1962 opinion the North Carolina Attorney General said tax listing abstracts are public records subject to public examination. 37 N.C.A.G. 85 (1962).

County tax assessors, after reviewing abstracts, may require people operating businesses in the county to submit a detailed inventory, statement of assets and liabilities, or other information pertinent to the discovery or appraisal of property taxable in the county. This additional information that is not expressly required to be shown in the abstract is not open to public inspection. This additional information is made available to the Department of Revenue upon request. Unauthorized disclosure of this information is a criminal offense.

Proposed Property Tax Appraisal Schedules, Standards and Rules - N.C. Gen. Stat. § 105-317(c)(1)

Boards of county commissioners review and approve values, standards and rules to be used in appraising property for taxes before January 1 of the year they are applied. The county tax assessor submits proposed schedules, standards and rules to the board at least 21 days before the meeting at which they will be considered by the board. On the same day they are submitted to the board, the assessor files a copy of the proposed schedules, standards and rules in his office, where they remain available for public inspection.

Taxpayer Information Held by State Agencies for Debt Collection - N.C. Gen. Stat. § 105A-15

Certain State agencies have access to taxpayer information from the Department of Revenue for the purposes of collecting debt. These agencies may use this information only for debt collection purposes. Disclosure for any other purposes is a criminal offense.

Agriculture Statistics - N.C. Gen. Stat. §§ 106-24 and 106-24.1

The Department of Agriculture compiles and publishes agriculture statistics. In doing so the Department must prevent the identification of information received from individual farm operators. This information is to be kept confidential by the Department. However, individual farm operator information collected for the purposes of the Department's animal health programs may be disclosed by the State Veterinarian when disclosure will assist in implementing these programs.

Information Obtained under the Food, Drug and Cosmetic Act - N.C. Gen. Stat. § 106-122(14)

The Department of Agriculture and the Board of Agriculture regulate food, drugs and cosmetics. In carrying out these duties, the Department and Board may obtain trade secret information. It is a criminal offense for people to use or disclose this information except as authorized by law.

Those who obtain trade secret information pursuant to the Food, Drug and Cosmetic Act may not reveal that information other than to the Commissioner of Agriculture or authorized Department of Agriculture employees. Violating this provision is a criminal offense.

Reports of Leaf Tobacco Sold - N.C. Gen. Stat. § 106-458

Leaf tobacco warehouse proprietors are required to send monthly reports to the Commissioner of Agriculture stating the amount of tobacco sold in their warehouses during the preceding month. The Commissioner copies information from these reports into a book, which is open to public inspection. The Commissioner is also required to publish these reports in a department bulletin and in one or more tobacco journals.

Poultry Products Inspection Act Information - N.C. Gen. Stat. §§ 106-549.56(a)(5) and 106-549.68(c)(4)

The Commissioner of Agriculture investigates businesses under the North Carolina Poultry Products Inspections Act. It is a criminal offense for State employees to make any of this information public unless authorized by the Commissioner. It is also a criminal offense to reveal trade secrets learned of in the process of obtaining information.

However, in a 1971 opinion the North Carolina Attorney General said that meat inspection records of the Department of Agriculture are public records and must be open for inspection. 41 N.C.A.G. 468 (1971).

Commercial Fertilizer Grade-Tonnage Reports - N.C. Gen. Stat. § 106-677

All brands of commercial fertilizers must be registered with the Commissioner of Agriculture before being sold or distributed in the State. Registrants are required to file written statements with the Commissioner indicating the tonnage of each grade of fertilizer sold in the State. This Commissioner and Department of Agriculture employees must keep this information confidential.

Permission to Release Genetically Engineered Organisms - N.C. Gen. Stat. § 106-774

People or companies who wish to release or distribute genetically engineered organisms must get permission from the Genetic Engineering Review Board. To get permission, applicants must submit to the Board certain information about the organisms. Applicants may designate as confidential those portions of the information they believe are entitled to treatment as confidential business information. This information may not be revealed.

However, people who review the effects of a proposed release of an organism may petition the Board to provide them with undisclosed confidential business information if it is necessary to perform the review effectively. The Board may determine whether to disclose the information to petitioners.

The Board is required to publish notice and a brief description of proposed releases of genetically engineered organisms. In addition, documents submitted as part of the application (excluding any confidential business information) are available for public inspection and copying at or near the site of the proposed release and in the Board's offices.

Assessment on Hog Purchases - N.C. Gen. Stat. § 106-794

For the purposes of determining the amounts of assessments to be levied under the Pork Promotion Assessment Act, hog buyers are required to keep records of the number of hogs purchased and the dates of purchase. The Department of Agriculture may require that this purchase information be submitted to the Department. This information must be kept confidential by Department employees, and may not be disclosed except by court order.

Receipt of Public Assistance - N.C. Gen. Stat. §§ 108A-11, 108A-73, 108A-79(e)(4) and 108A-80

It is unlawful to disclose any list of names or other information about people who apply for or receive public assistance, except for the purposes of administering public assistance programs.

However, every month the Department of Human Resources is required to supply to county auditors copies of registers showing complete lists of recipients of Aid to Families with Dependent Children and State-County Special Assistance for Adults, which includes recipients' addresses and the amounts of monthly grants. This register is a public record and is open to public inspection during the regular office hours of the county auditor. This information may not be used for commercial or political purposes. It is a criminal offense to use this information for these purposes.

Listings of recipients of benefits under any public assistance or social services program used for official purposes by county boards or departments of social services may not be used as a mailing list for political purposes. It is a criminal offense to use this information for these purposes.

People (and their representatives) who appeal decisions of county Departments of Social Services concerning the receipt of public assistance may inspect their case files before and during their appeals. However, portions of the file unrelated to the appeal, or information in the file that is required by federal or state law to be kept confidential, may not be disclosed to appellants.

Members of county boards of social services may inspect public assistance and social services records in social services offices, but they may not disclose or make public any information they acquire by examining those records.

In a 1969 opinion the North Carolina Attorney General confirmed that the county auditor's register of aid recipients is a public record, and that any person may copy it regardless of what they wish to use it for. The county auditor is under no obligation to inform people about the uses they may or may not make of the list. 40 N.C.A.G. 709 (1969).

In a 1969 opinion the North Carolina Attorney General said Departments of

Social Services were allowed to supply names, addresses, sex, dates of birth, and other information on children receiving AFDC benefits to a nonprofit group commissioned to do a survey of children's services. This disclosure was considered consistent with "administering public assistance programs." 40 N.C.A.G. 713 (1969).

In a 1979 opinion the North Carolina Attorney General said Departments of Social Services were allowed to release records of Title XX public assistance recipients to the Evaluation Section of the Department of Human Resources in order for that section to conduct a study requested by the General Assembly. This disclosure was considered consistent with "administering public assistance programs." 49 N.C.A.G. 61 (1979).

In a 1980 opinion the North Carolina Attorney General said Departments of Social Services were not allowed to release protective service case records of juveniles to a volunteer advisory group appointed by the Chief District Court Judge to advise the juvenile court about custody of children in foster homes. This disclosure was not considered consistent with "administering public assistance programs." 49 N.C.A.G. 198 (1980).

In a 1984 opinion the North Carolina Attorney General said that law enforcement officers may have access to public assistance records at Department of Social Services offices, without subpoenas, search warrants or court orders, to investigate allegations of criminal fraud by recipients in obtaining assistance. This disclosure was considered consistent with "administering public assistance programs." 53 N.C.A.G. 108 (1984).

Day Care Inspection Plans - N.C. Gen. Stat. § 110-105 and § 110-105.1

The Child Day-Care Commission is required to adopt plans for routine inspections of all day care facilities and unannounced inspections of randomly selected registered day care homes. These plans are confidential unless a court orders disclosure.

Child Support - Location of Absent Parents - N.C. Gen. Stat. § 110-139 and § 110-139.1

The Department of Human Resources is responsible for attempting to locate absent parents for the purpose of establishing paternity of dependent children or securing support for them. In doing so, the Department obtains information from government agencies and private employers. State, county and municipal agencies are required to provide this information to the Department even if the information is otherwise made confidential by law.[28] The Department keeps information on child

---

In a 1979 opinion the North Carolina Attorney General said that State, county and municipal personnel directors must release confidential information about their employees to the Department of Human Resources to aid it in child support enforcement efforts. 48 N.C.A.G. 85 (1979)

custody and the unlawful taking or restraint of children.

All non-judicial records the Department keeps on these subjects are confidential, and may not be disclosed except to certain agencies and legislative committees dealing with parental location and child support.

Aid to the Needy Blind - N.C. Gen. Stat. § 111-28

The Department of Human Resources receives and keeps information about needy blind people related to their application for, and receipt of, financial aid from the Department. The Department may not disclose any of this information except in the administration of the financial aid program.

The Department may release certain recipient information to the Department of Revenue and the Division of Motor Vehicles for use in administering their laws. These agencies must otherwise keep the information confidential.

Marine Fisheries Commission Records - N.C. Gen. Stat. § 113-163

The Marine Fisheries Commission may require fishing licensees to keep certain records to assist the Commission in carrying out its duties and conservation policy. These records must be exhibited to representatives of the Department of Environment, Health and Natural Resources upon request. These records are not public records and may not be disclosed except with a court order.

The Department may compile statistical data that do not identify individual licensees. This information is public record open to inspection and examination by any person.

Coastal Fisheries - Referenda for Assessments - N.C. Gen. Stat. § 113-315.3

Agencies representing the fishing industry may petition the Marine Fisheries Commission for permission to hold referenda among coastal fisheries for the purposes of levying an assessment to be used in the promotion of the fishing industry.

If the Commission certifies an agency to conduct a referendum, the agency must open and count ballots in a public meeting, and it must declare the results publicly.

Coastal Land-Use Plans - N.C. Gen. Stat. § 113A-110(e) and (g)

Coastal counties prepare land-use plans to regulate land and water use in accordance with State guidelines and environmental concerns. These plans are prepared by the Coastal Resources Commission, the county, or a designated lead regional organization. Before these plans are adopted, copies of proposed plans must be made available for public inspection in the county courthouse during designated hours. Copies of adopted plans must be made available for public inspection by the county, the Commission and the lead regional organization.

Areas of Environmental Concern - N.C. Gen. Stat. § 113A-115(a)(1)

The Secretary of the Department of Environment, Health and Natural Resources designates certain coastal areas as areas of environmental concern. Before doing so, the Secretary must make a description of the proposed area available for public inspection in the county courthouse of each county affected.

Forest Product Assessments - N.C. Gen. Stat. § 113A-195(e) and (f)

The Secretary of Revenue may levy assessments on processors of primary forest products. In the process of levying and collecting these assessments, the Secretary gets forest product production reports from processors. These reports are used only for administration and collection of assessments, and are not otherwise public records. It is a criminal offense for State employees or officials to disclose this information.

Energy Information Reporting System - N.C. Gen. Stat. § 113B-10(c)

The Energy Policy Council serves as a central repository for information on energy-related matters. The Council is responsible for an information reporting system for use by government agencies and the public.

Division of Criminal Information - N.C. Gen. Stat. § 114-110

The Division of Criminal Information in the Department of Justice collects and correlates information about crimes to assist law enforcement agencies in performing their duties. This information includes motor vehicle registration, drivers' licenses, wanted and missing persons, stolen property, warrants, stolen vehicles, firearms registration, drugs, drug users and parole and probation histories. The Division makes this information available only to those who require it for justice administration.

Criminal Record Checks of School Employees - N.C. Gen. Stat. § 114-19.2(a) and (c1)

The Department of Justice may provide criminal background checks of applicants and employees of public schools and schools within the Department of Human Resources, if the applicant or employee consents. Local school boards and the Department must keep the criminal background information they receive confidential as personnel information.

Criminal Record Checks of Employees of Hospitals, Nursing Homes, Mental Health Authorities, and Mental Health Contract Agencies - N.C. Gen. Stat. § 114-19.3

The Department of Justice may provide criminal background checks of applicants and employees of public hospitals, nursing homes, area mental health, developmental disabilities, and substance abuse authorities or their contract agencies, if the applicant or employee consents. The organization or agency receiving this information from the Department of Justice must keep the information confidential.

Elementary and Secondary Education

Elementary and Secondary Education - Public Records - N.C. Gen. Stat. § 115C-3

Except as otherwise provided, access to information collected or made under the Elementary and Secondary Education Act (N.C. Gen. Stat. § 115C) must be in conformity with the public records law.

In a 1973 opinion the North Carolina Attorney General said that teacher contracts are public records. 42 N.C.A.G. 229 (1973).

Elementary and Secondary Education - Open Meetings - N.C. Gen. Stat. § 115C-4

Meetings of governmental bodies held pursuant to the Elementary and Secondary Education Act (N.C. Gen. Stat. §115C) must be in conformity with the open meetings law.

In *Jacksonville Daily News Co. v. Onslow County Bd. of Educ.*, 113 N.C. App. 127, 439 S.E.2d 607 (1993), the North Carolina Court of Appeals ruled that a school board violated N.C. Gen. Stat. §115C-4 when it deliberated and decided in private telephone conversations among board members and in a closed session of the board to give its members retroactive pay raises.

In a 1985 opinion the North Carolina Attorney General said that a local board of education does not have to state in a public record or in a public meeting the reasons why it decided not to renew a teacher's contract. The reasons may be included in a teacher's personnel file, which is confidential. 54 N.C.A.G. 84 (1985).

Proceedings of State Board of Education - N.C. Gen. Stat. § 115C-11

All proceedings of the State Board of Education are recorded, and the records are kept in the office of the Superintendent of Public Instruction. These records are open to public inspection.

All Board voting is by voice vote unless a secret ballot is demanded by any member. Voting on textbook adoptions must be by recorded vote

Uniform Education Reporting System - N.C. Gen. Stat. § 115C-12(18)(c)

The State Board of Education works with institutions of higher learning in the State to develop information and statistics on the acceptance of public school students into higher education institutions and their progress in these institutions. The Board requires local boards of education to provide this information, except confidential information, to parents of public school students, and to make this information available to the general public.

Confidentiality of Information Obtained by the Superintendent of Public Instruction, the Department of Public Instruction and the State Board of Education - N.C. Gen. Stat. § 115C-13

Local boards of education are required to provide certain information to the Superintendent of Public Instruction and the State Board of Education. It is a criminal offense for the Superintendent, the Board, and employees of the Department of Public Instruction to disclose information that local boards and their officers and employees may not disclose.

Registry of Textbook Publisher Representatives - N.C. Gen. Stat. § 115C-94

Publishers who submit textbooks for adoption by the State Board of Education for public instruction in North Carolina must register their authorized representatives in the office of the Superintendent of Public Instruction. This registration list is open to the public for inspection.

Textbook lists submitted by departments of North Carolina State University to the university bookstore are public records, and these lists are available for inspection by private textbook vendors. 41 N.C.A.G. 199 (1971).

Census of Children with Special Needs - N.C. Gen. Stat. § 115C-110(j)

The State Board of Education takes an annual census of children with special needs. This census is made available to the public no later than January 15 each year.

Records Relating to Children with Special Needs - N.C. Gen. Stat. § 115C-114

Local educational agencies may not release records, data or information on children with special needs except to the eligible student, his parents or guardian or any surrogate parent, or certain specified school officials and representatives of government agencies.

Parents, guardians and surrogate parents have the right to add information to these records and to have outdated, incorrect, misleading or irrelevant information expunged.

Classification of Children with Special Needs - N.C. Gen. Stat. § 115C-116(g)

Decisions regarding the classification of children with special needs by local educational agencies may be reviewed in administrative hearings. These hearings are closed to the public unless the parent, guardian or surrogate parent requests in writing that the hearing be open to the public.

Statewide Student Testing Program Scores - N.C. Gen. Stat. § 115C-174.13

Any written material containing the identifiable scores of individual students on tests under the statewide testing program is not a public record and may not be made public, except under the federal Family Education and Privacy Rights Act.

Outcome-Based Education Program - N.C. Gen. Stat. § 115C-238.14(c)(8)

The Department of Public Instruction approves and oversees local projects under its Outcome-Based Education Program. These projects are to be shared with the public. Annual reports describing program goals, activities and accomplishments are made available to the public.

Minutes of Local Boards of Education - N.C. Gen. Stat. § 115C-276(b)

Superintendents of public schools are responsible for recording the minutes of school board meetings and keeping the minutes in the board's office, where they are open at all times to public inspection.

Public School Teacher Complaint/Commendation Files - N.C. Gen. Stat. § 115C-325(b)

Public school superintendents keep in their offices a file for each teacher containing complaints, commendations or suggestions for correction or improvement about the teacher's professional conduct. This file is open for the teacher's inspection at all reasonable times, but others may inspect the file only in accordance with rules adopted by the school board.

Public School Student Records - N.C. Gen. Stat. § 115C-402

The official records of public school students are kept in the schools after they graduate or should have graduated. These records are not public records and are not subject to inspection pursuant to the public records law.

Community College Records and Meetings - N.C. Gen. Stat. §§ 115D-78 and 115D-79

All rules, regulations and public records of the State Board of Community Colleges, the Department of Community Colleges, and local boards of trustees of community colleges are available for inspection and reproduction on payment of fees by any person, in accordance with the public records law.

All official meetings of the State Board of Community Colleges and of local boards of trustees are open to the public in accordance with the open meetings law.

University of North Carolina Health-Care Liability Insurance Records - N.C. Gen. Stat. § 116-222

The Board of Governors of the University of North Carolina may purchase insurance or create a self-insurance program for coverage of its health-care providers against claims of personal tort liability. Records on this liability insurance program are not public records. They are also not subject to discovery under the Rules of Civil Procedure.

List of Escheated and Abandoned Property - N.C. Gen. Stat. § 116B-30

The State Treasurer delivers a list of escheated and abandoned property to each clerk of superior court by November 1 of each year. At that time the Treasurer publishes a notice that he has done so in newspapers with statewide circulation.

The clerks of superior court keep these property lists permanently in their offices. For six months after the Treasurer's notice, the lists of owners of the properties and the supporting data may be confidential. This does not apply to owners of reported property making inquiries about their property.

The lists kept in the clerks' offices on a permanent basis are available for public inspection.

Records of Property Deposited to Escheat Fund - N.C. Gen. Stat. § 116B-36(i)

Some of the proceeds from the disposition of escheated and abandoned property are deposited in an Escheat Fund. Before making a deposit to the Escheat Fund, or before retaining or destroying property, the State Treasurer makes a record containing certain information about the property and its ownership. These records are available for public inspection at all reasonable business hours.

Property Records Inspected by State Treasurer and Commissioner of Insurance in Administration of Abandoned Property - N.C. Gen. Stat. § 116B-39(c)

The State Treasurer and the Commissioner of Insurance may inspect any records relating to property that must be reported pursuant to the escheats and abandoned property law. These records are confidential and not available for public inspection to the extent the Treasurer and Commissioner find it necessary to keep them confidential to protect the interest of the property holder, the property owner, the State and the public welfare. Any of these records that are confidential under State or federal law are also not available for public inspection.

Certification of Holdings of Unclaimed and Abandoned Property - N.C. Gen. Stat. § 116B-49(b)

Business associations holding unclaimed and abandoned property are required to certify their holdings on tax returns or on a separate form to the Secretary of

Revenue. These certifications are not privileged or confidential, and this information is furnished to the Escheat Fund yearly.

Legislator Access to State Agency Information - N.C. Gen. Stat. § 120-19

State agencies, officials and employees are required to provide to members of the General Assembly, upon request, all information and data that is in their possession or that is ascertainable from their records. A member of the General Assembly requesting the information need not be a member of a General Assembly committee investigating an issue in order to have access to the information. 48 N.C.A.G. 84 (1979).

The only exception is taxpayer information. State offices having taxpayer records are only required to provide sample tax returns to the Fiscal Research Division of the General Assembly upon request, and the taxpayers' names and identifying information must be deleted from the forms before disclosure. N.C. Gen. Stat. § 105-259.

Lobbyist Expense Reports - N.C. Gen. Stat. §§ 120-47.6(c) and 120-47.7(c)

Lobbyists and their principals are required to file lobbying expense reports with the Secretary of State after each session of the General Assembly. These reports are open to public inspection.

Disclosure of Confidential Information by Legislators Forbidden - N.C. Gen. Stat. § 120-87

Legislators may not disclose or use confidential information they obtain in their official capacities for the financial gain of themselves, their businesses, their household members, or others.

General Assembly Candidates' Statements of Economic Interest - N.C. Gen. Stat. § 120-94

Candidates for the General Assembly are required to file statements of economic interest containing various information about their finances and business interests. These statements are public records and are available for public inspection and copying during normal business hours at county boards of election, the Legislative Library, and the Legislative Services Office. If the county board of elections has no office, the statements are available for inspection and copying at the office of the clerk of superior court.

Legislative Ethics Committee - N.C. Gen. Stat. § 120-103(b) and (d1)

The Legislative Ethics Committee of the General Assembly investigates violations of the Legislative Ethics Act (N.C. Gen. Stat., Chapter 120, Article 14) or criminal violations by legislators while acting in their official capacity.

The Committee may hold hearings as part of these inquiries. The Committee may, in its discretion, hold hearings in a closed session. The person under investigation may demand in writing that a hearing be either open or closed.

Among the actions the Committee may take, it may dismiss a complaint or issue a private or public admonishment to a legislator. In the case of a dismissal or private admonishment, the Committee keeps its records or findings in confidence, unless the legislator requests that they be made public. If the Committee later finds that a legislator's subsequent unethical activities were similar to and the subject of an earlier private admonishment then the Committee may make public the earlier admonishment and the records and findings relating to it.

Communications Between Legislators and Legislative Employees - N.C. Gen. Stat. §§ 120-130, 120-131, 120-132, 120-133, and 120-134

A request from a legislator to a legislative employee to draft a bill is confidential. The identity of the legislator and the existence of the request may not be revealed to any person except other legislative employees without the consent of the legislator.

A request from a legislator to a legislative employee for information is confidential. The identity of the legislator and the existence of the request may not be revealed to any person except other legislative employees without the consent of the legislator. The Fiscal Research Division of the Legislative Services Office may publish lists of information requests without revealing the names of individual legislators making the requests.

Documents submitted to legislative employees by legislators in connection with drafting or information requests are confidential.

Documents prepared by legislative employees at the request of legislators are confidential and may not be revealed to any person except other legislative employees without the consent of the legislator. These documents become available to the public when they are introduced as bills or resolutions, when they are proposed as amendments or substitutes for bills, when they are offered as proposed conference committee reports, or when they are distributed at an open committee meeting or session. Documents that are not made available to the public in one of these ways are not public records.

Legislative employees may not be required to disclose any confidential legislative information or information they obtained in the legislative meetings and sessions. However, a judge may order an employee to disclose this information if it is necessary for the proper administration of justice.

Drafting and information requests to legislative employees and documents prepared by legislative employees concerning redistricting become public records when the redistricting act they pertain to is ratified.

Violations of these provisions are grounds for disciplinary action against employees and removal of public officers. There is no criminal penalty.

Legislative Assessment Reports for New Licensing Boards - N.C. Gen. Stat. § 120-149.3

Before the General Assembly may study or create a new licensing board, the Legislative Committee on New Licensing Boards must conduct a study of the need and impact of the proposed board. The Committee issues preliminary, final and supplementary reports with its assessment. These reports are kept in the Legislative Library for public inspection.

Inspection of Archived Public Records - N.C. Gen. Stat. § 121-4(3)

The Department of Cultural Resources preserves public records and historical documents in the North Carolina State Archives. The Department must permit inspection, examination and copying of these documents at reasonable times under the Department's supervision, subject to special terms or conditions restricting their use.

North Carolina Housing Finance Agency Bond Issues - N.C. Gen. Stat. § 122A-8.1

The State Treasurer issues bonds and notes authorized by the North Carolina Housing Finance Agency. The Treasurer employs and designates financial consultants, underwriters and bond attorneys associated with the bond issue. The Treasurer conducts a formal performance evaluation of these people after each bond issue. This performance evaluation is open to public inspection.

Confidential Information Relating to Clients at Facilities for People with Mental Illnesses, Developmental Disabilities, and Substance Abuse Problems - N.C. Gen. Stat. §§ 122C-3(9), 122C-25, 122C-30, 122C-52, 122C-53, 122C-53, 122C-54, 122C-55, 122C-56, 122C-186, 122C-191, 122C-192, 122C-205, 122C-207, 122C-224.3, 122C-267, 122C-268, 122C-268.1, 122C-286.

Chapter 122C of the General Statutes regulates facilities that provide services for the care, treatment, habilitation or rehabilitation of people with mental illnesses, developmental disabilities, and substance abuse problems.

Much of the client information at these facilities is confidential, is exempt from the public records law, and may not be disclosed to the general public. N.C. Gen. Stat. § 122C-52.

The following summarizes several of the confidentiality provisions and the limited circumstances in which disclosure of confidential information is permitted.

Written and other information received by facilities concerning their clients and received in connection with the performance of any function of the facility is confidential information. This does not include statistical information about treatment services shared for training, treatment, habilitation or monitoring purposes that does not identify clients. N.C. Gen. Stat. § 122C-3(9).

The Secretary of the Department of Human Resources inspects these facilities, and in doing so has access to confidential and privileged client information. The Secretary and Department employees may not disclose any confidential or privileged information to unauthorized people without consent of clients or the clients' representatives. They also may not disclose the name of anyone who has provided information about the facility without that person's consent. This information is not a public record. Unauthorized disclosure is a criminal offense. N.C. Gen. Stat. §§ 122C-25 and 122C-192.

At hospitals licensed for treating people with mental illnesses, developmental disabilities and substance abuse problems, and at area authorities and State facilities providing this treatment, the proceedings of peer review committees, the materials and records they produce and the materials they consider are confidential and are not public records. N.C. Gen. Stat. §§ 122C-30 and 122C-191.

Under limited circumstances, facilities may disclose confidential information to clients, to their next of kin, their legally responsible persons, to their internal client advocates, and to attorneys.[29] N.C. Gen. Stat. § 122C-53.

A facility must disclose confidential client information if ordered to do so by a court.[30] If a facility has been ordered to conduct a mental examination of a criminal defendant, the facility may send the results of the examination to the court and the attorneys. Facilities may, in some circumstances, provide confidential information to staff attorneys with the Attorney General's office and to attorneys representing facilities and facility employees. Facilities are required to report cases of child abuse and elder abuse to Departments of Social Services, and they must provide relevant confidential information when making these reports. N.C. Gen. Stat. § 122C-54.

In a variety of circumstances, facilities may disclose confidential information to other facilities and other care providers for the care and treatment of clients. Facilities may provide certain confidential information to the Department of Corrections for the treatment of inmates. Facilities may provide confidential information to certain government agencies if necessary to establish financial benefits for clients. Facilities

---

In a 1976 opinion the North Carolina Attorney General said special counsel representing a patient at a facility is entitled to inspect and receive copies of the patient's records, including medical charts. The opinion also said that facility personnel are entitled to supervise counsel's inspection of records, and they may establish reasonable time, place, and surrounding circumstances for inspection. 46 N.C.A.G. 142 (1976)

In a 1971 opinion the North Carolina Attorney General said that facilities must also disclose this information if ordered to do so by a clerk of court. 41 N.C.A.G. 666 (1971)

may provide some confidential information to certain family members or others if necessary for treatment, or to inform them of client diagnoses and prognoses. N.C. Gen. Stat. § 122C-55.

In order the assist in preparing statistical reports and to assist in evaluation, research, auditing and financial planning, facilities may provide certain confidential information to other government agencies. N.C. Gen. Stat. § 122C-56.

Although members of the General Assembly are ex officio visitors at all State facilities providing care and treatment for clients, legislators do not have the right to have access to confidential client information. N.C. Gen. Stat. § 122C-186.

When certain clients either escape from facilities or breach the conditions of release from facilities, the facilities are required to notify law enforcement agencies in order to locate and return these clients. In notifying law enforcement agencies, facilities may provide a limited amount of confidential client information sufficient to ensure the return of the client and the public's safety. N.C. Gen. Stat. § 122C-205.

Court records made in admission and discharge proceedings are confidential and are not open to the general public except as ordered by the court. N.C. Gen. Stat. § 122C-207.

The General Statutes say that facilities are required to disclose confidential information if ordered to do so by a court. The statutes provide for hearing procedures for getting court orders. N.C. Gen. Stat. § 122C-54.

However, federal law and regulations also restrict the circumstances in which North Carolina facilities receiving federal funding may disclose confidential information. These regulations take precedence over state law for federally assisted facilities. The federal regulations provide stricter judicial procedures for ordering disclosure of confidential client information. See, 42 U.S.C. § 290-dd2 and 42 C.F.R. § 2.65. In particular, the procedures for requiring facilities to provide client information to law enforcement agencies investigating facility clients are more restrictive.

Judicial Review of Admissions to Facilities For Treatment of Mental Illness or Substance Abuse - N.C. Gen. Stat. §§ 122C-224.3, 122C-267, 122C-268, 122C-268.1, and 122C-286

Judicial hearings reviewing admissions and commitments of people to facilities for treatment of mental illness and substance abuse are either open or closed, depending on the circumstances.

The following review hearings are closed, unless the patient requests that the hearing be open:

(1) Hearings to review voluntary admissions of minors to 24-hour facilities

when in need of treatment for mental illness or substance abuse (N.C. Gen Stat. § 122C-224.3(d));

(2) Involuntary inpatient or outpatient commitments to 24-hour facilities of people who are mentally ill and dangerous to themselves or others, or people who are mentally retarded and because of an accompanying behavior disorder are dangerous to others (N.C. Gen. Stat. §§ 122C-267(f) and 122C-268(h)); and

(3) Involuntary commitments to 24-hour facilities of substance abusers who are dangerous to themselves or others (N.C. Gen. Stat. § 122C-286(f)).

A hearing to review the commitment to a 24-hour facility of a person found not guilty of a criminal charge by reason of insanity is open to the public. N.C. Gen. Stat. § 122C-268.1(g).

In *In re Hayes* 111 N.C. App. 384, 432 S.E.2d 862 (1993), the North Carolina Court of Appeals held that requiring open commitment hearings for insanity acquitees, while requiring the closing of other commitment hearings, did not violate the defendant's equal protection rights. The Court said an insanity acquittee is entitled to fewer constitutional protections than an individual who is civilly committed. The Court said the public has a right to know when and if an insanity acquittee is discharged into the community.

In *WSOC Television, Inc. v. State ex rel. Attorney General, (In re Belk)* 107 N.C. App. 448, 420 S.E.2d 682 (1992), the North Carolina Court of Appeals upheld the constitutionality of the statute making involuntary commitment hearings confidential. The Court ruled that there was no constitutional right for a television station or the public to have access to an involuntary commitment hearing or the records of the person who was the subject of the hearing.

State Libraries and State Publications - N.C. Gen. Stat. §§ 125-11.6, 125-11.7, 125-11.8, 125-11.9, and 125-11.10

State agencies are required to send copies of each of their State publications to the State Publications Clearinghouse. With some exceptions for internal, administrative, and otherwise confidential documents (N.C. Gen. Stat. § 125-11.6(4)), State publications are any documents prepared by a State agency or private agency under contract with a State agency or under the supervision of a State agency.

The State Clearinghouse distributes State publications to depository libraries around the State, where they are accessible to the public.

Library User Records - N.C. Gen. Stat. §§ 125-18 and 125-19

No public libraries or private libraries open to the public may disclose any records identifying people who requested or got materials, information or services from the library, or people who used the library.

However, library user records may be disclosed: 1) with the consent of the user; 2) as necessary for library operation; 3) in response to a subpoena or court order; or 4) as required by law.

Personnel Records of Government Employees - N.C. Gen. Stat. §§ 126-22, 153A-98, 160A-168, 115C-321, 115D-29, 122C-158, 130A-42, 131E-97.1, and 162A-6.1

Several statutes regulate public disclosure of personnel information of government employees. With slight variations, personnel files of state employees,[31] county employees,[32] municipal employees,[33] public school employees,[34] community college employees,[35] employees of mental health area authorities,[36] employees of district health departments,[37] public hospital employees,[38] and employees of water and sewer authorities[39] are subject to these disclosure rules.

These rules apply to personnel information for applicants, current employees, and former employees.

With certain exceptions, personnel information gathered by government agency employers is confidential and may not be disclosed. Personnel information that

---

N.C. Gen. Stat. § 126-22, et. seq. The rules governing the confidentiality of state employees' personnel files also apply to employees of area mental health, mental retardation and substance abuse authorities, local social services departments, public health departments, and local emergency management agencies receiving federal grant-in-aid funds. N.C. Gen. Stat. § 126-5)

N.C. Gen. Stat. § 153A-98

N.C. Gen. Stat. § 160A-168

N.C. Gen. Stat. § 115C-321

N.C. Gen. Stat. § 115D-29

N.C. Gen. Stat. § 122C-158

N.C. Gen. Stat. § 130A-42

N.C. Gen. Stat. § 131E-97.1

N.C. Gen. Stat. § 162A-6.1

agencies may not disclose includes information about an individual's:

(1) application;

(2) selection or nonselection;

(3) promotions;

(4) demotions;

(5) transfers;

(6) leave;

(7) salary;

(8) suspension;

(9) performance;

(10) disciplinary actions; and

(11) termination.

In special circumstances, a government employer's chief management official may disclose some of this otherwise confidential information. If the official determines that it is essential for maintaining the agency's integrity or the level or quality of services of the agency, the official may disclose information about an employee's:

(1) employment, reinstatement or nonemployment;

(2) promotion or demotion;

(3) suspension;

(4) other disciplinary action (county or municipal employees only, not state employees);

(5) transfer; and

(6) termination.

Before releasing this otherwise confidential information for inspection, the official must write a memo explaining the reasons for releasing the information, and the memo must be placed in the employee's personnel file.

Confidential personnel information about government employees may also be inspected in other limited circumstances. Employees and supervisors may see much of this information, and some other government agencies may inspect this information. State agencies are required to provide personnel information, upon request, to members of the General Assembly. N.C. Gen. Stat. § 120-19; 48 N.C.A.G. 84 (1979). However, for the most part this information may not be divulged to assist in a criminal prosecution or a tax investigation of an employee. For details on the release of confidential personnel information in these circumstances, consult the statutes cited above.

Although most government personnel information is confidential, government agencies are required to keep a record and allow public inspection of certain employment information about each of their employees. These public records must contain the following information about each employee:

(1) name;

(2) age;

(3) date of original employment or appointment to service with the governmental jurisdiction;

(4) current position;

(5) title;

(6) current salary;

(7) date and amount of most recent salary increase or decrease;

(8) date of most recent promotion, demotion, transfer, suspension, separation, or other change in position classification; and

(9) office or station to which the employee is currently assigned.

For public hospital employees, the public information also includes beginning and ending dates of employment, position title, position descriptions, and total compensation of current *and* former positions. Also, for licensed medical providers employed by or having privileges to practice in a public hospital, the following information is public: educational history and qualifications, date and jurisdiction of original and current licensure, and information about medical board certifications or other qualifications of medical specialists.[40]

In *News & Observer Pub. Co. v. Poole,* 330 N.C. 465, 412 S.E.2d 7 (1992), the North Carolina Supreme Court emphasized that State employee personnel information

---

N.C. Gen. Stat. § 131E-97.1

is confidential only when it is first gathered by the State agency for which an employee works. N.C. Gen. Stat. § 126-22. In *Poole*, the State Bureau of Investigation (SBI) investigated certain State employees. The Court ruled that information obtained by the SBI from sources other than the employer was not confidential because it was not gathered by the State employees' agency. On the other hand, any information gathered first by the agency and turned over to the SBI was confidential.

In *Elkin Tribune v. Yadkin County Board of Commissioners*, 331 N.C. 734, 417 S.E.2d 465 (1992), the North Carolina Supreme Court ruled that applications for county manager were confidential applicant information not subject to disclosure, pursuant to N.C. Gen. Stat. § 153A-98. See *State v. McKoy*, 331 N.C. 731 also.

In *Durham Herald Co. v. County of Durham*, 334 N.C. 677, 435 S.E.2d 317 (1993), the North Carolina Supreme Court ruled that applications from people who applied to replace a resigning sheriff were confidential applicant information not subject to disclosure, pursuant to N.C. Gen. Stat. § 153A-98.

In a 1976 opinion the North Carolina Attorney General said that the State Personnel Commission may not use a closed session to deliberate upon and approve a county's plan to deviate from the Commission's standard salary ranges. 46 N.C.A.G. 20 (1976).

In a 1977 opinion the North Carolina Attorney General said that a State agency may not inform the news media that a State employee is being investigated. The news media also may not be told why an employee is being investigated or the results of the investigation. The news media may be informed that the agency has internal administrative procedures for investigating complaints against its employees, and the media may be informed what those procedures are.

The Attorney General said that if an employee is suspended, the agency must disclose that the employee was suspended and the date of the suspension (for the employee's most recent suspension, only). However, the agency may not disclose the type of suspension (for example, suspension with pay or without pay) or the reason for it. If an employee is suspended pending an investigation, the agency may not disclose the fact that the suspension is pending an investigation. The agency also may not disclose whether the investigation is internal or is being conducted by an outside agency, such as a law enforcement agency. 47 N.C.A.G. 141 (1977).

In a 1978 opinion, the North Carolina Attorney General said that information disclosed at a State employee's departmental private hearing could not be disclosed to the media because the hearing is private. On the other hand, information disclosed at a State employee's appeal hearing before the State Personnel Commission may be disclosed to the media because the hearing is public.

The Attorney General said that the nature of discipline taken against a State employee may not be disclosed to the media unless it is made public at a hearing before the State Personnel Commission. Otherwise, the employing agency may disclose only the fact and date of an employee's most recent demotion, suspension, separation or other change in position or classification. 47 N.C.A.G. 164 (1978).

In a 1979 opinion the North Carolina Attorney General said that State, county and municipal personnel directors must release confidential information about their employees to the Department of Human Resources to aid it in child support enforcement efforts, pursuant to N.C. Gen. Stat. § 110-139. 48 N.C.A.G. 85 (1979).

In a 1983 opinion the North Carolina Attorney General said that home addresses of State employees may be obtained from State personnel offices by ad valorem tax collectors pursuant to N.C. Gen. Stat. §105-368(i). This kind of disclosure does not violate the prohibition in N.C. Gen. Stat. §126-24(5) against release of personnel information for assisting in tax investigations. Ad valorem tax collectors do not engage in investigations to determine tax liability. They only collect taxes, the taxpayer's liability for taxes already having been determined by the tax assessor. 52 N.C.A.G. 85 (1983).

In a 1985 opinion the North Carolina Attorney General said that a local board of education need not state in a public record or in a public meeting the reasons why it decided not to renew a teacher's contract. The reasons may be included in a teacher's personnel file, which is confidential. 54 N.C.A.G. 84 (1985).

National Guard Records - N.C. Gen. Stat. § 127A-17.1

No records of the national guard may be disclosed or used for anything except official purposes, and no records may be disclosed, destroyed or used in violation of federal law.

Military Surplus Registers - N.C. Gen. Stat. § 127A-131

People or companies buying goods and equipment for resale, which may reasonably be thought to be the property of the armed forces, are required to keep registers of their purchases. These registers must include information on the goods purchased and on the people and companies who sell the goods to the buyers. These registers are open to the inspection of the public at all times.

Local Governmental Employees' Retirement System - N.C. Gen. Stat. § 128-28(j) and (q)

The Board of Trustees of the North Carolina Local Governmental Employees' Retirement System keeps records of all its proceedings. These records are open to public inspection.

Government agencies that keep lists of names and addresses in administering their retirement programs may upon request provide to the Retirement System information limited to social security numbers and current names and addresses of members and beneficiaries. This information is confidential, and it may be used only to inform beneficiaries of their rights to accruals of benefits. Unauthorized disclosure is a criminal offense. Violations may also subject public officials to dismissal.

Medical Records in the Public Health System - N.C. Gen. Stat. § 130A-12

All privileged patient medical records in the possession of the Department of Environment, Health and Natural Resources and local health departments are confidential and are not public records.

In a 1958 opinion the North Carolina Attorney General said that clinical records of individual patients treated in public health departments are not public records and are not subject to public inspection. 34 N.C.A.G. 132 (1958). However, in a separate opinion the Attorney General said that documents, papers and letters other than clinical records accumulated by local health officers and health department are public records. 34 N.C.A.G. 132 (1958).

Birth Certificates - N.C. Gen. Stat. §§ 130A-99 and 130A-102

Birth certificates are filed with each county's register of deeds. They are also on file with the State Registrar of Vital Statistics. Birth certificates are open to inspection and examination. Copies are provided to any person upon request. Certified copies are provided only to:

(1) A person requesting his own certificate or the certificate of a spouse, child, parent, brother or sister;

(2) A person seeking information for a legal determination of personal or property rights; or

(3) An authorized representative or attorney of these people.

Communicable Diseases - N.C. Gen. Stat. § 130A-143

All information and records identifying that a person has AIDS virus infection or that he has or may have other diseases or conditions that must be reported under the communicable diseases law (N.C. Gen. Stat. Chapter 130A, Article 6) is strictly confidential. This information may not be released or made public except under 11 circumstances listed in the statute. Some of these circumstances include disclosure with consent, for treatment, for statistical purposes, for controlling the spread of communicable diseases or conditions, for research, and pursuant to subpoena or court order.

In *Weston v. Carolina Medicorp*, 102 N.C. App. 370, 402 S.E.2d 653 (1991), the North Carolina Court of Appeals ruled that a hospital could require doctors admitting patients who are HIV positive to place those patients on blood and body fluid isolation, which identifies a patient as potentially HIV infectious. The Court found that the hospital's rule was justified by N.C. Gen. Stat. § 130-143(3), which permits release of information about patient HIV infection to health care personnel providing medical care to the patient.

Cancer Registry - N.C. Gen. Stat. § 130A-212

The Department of Environment, Health and Natural Resources keeps a central registry of cancer patients. The clinical records or reports of individual patients are confidential and are not public records open to inspection.

Solid Waste Management - N.C. Gen. Stat. § 130A-304

The Department of Environment, Health and Natural Resources licenses, regulates and inspects facilities that dispose and treat solid waste. The following information received or prepared by the Department in carrying out these functions is confidential and is not subject to disclosure under the public records law:

(1) Information deemed by the Secretary to be a trade secret;

(2) Information that is confidential under federal or state law; and

(3) Information compiled in anticipation of enforcement or criminal proceedings, but only if disclosure would interfere with the institution of those proceedings.

Confidential information may be disclosed to other State or federal agencies to carry out functions of the Department or the other agencies. Unauthorized disclosure is a criminal offense.

State Center for Health Statistics - N.C. Gen. Stat. § 130A-374

The State Center for Health Statistics collects health data. Medical records of individual patients are confidential and are not public records open to inspection. The Center may disclose this information if the patient authorizes disclosure or for bona fide research purposes.

Autopsies - N.C. Gen. Stat. § 130A-389

Autopsies may be ordered by medical examiners, or requested by district attorneys and superior court judges if they believe it is advisable and in the public interest. In these circumstances, autopsy reports are submitted to the Chief Medical Examiner. Copies of these autopsy reports are available to others upon request.

In deaths where an autopsy is not officially ordered or requested, the Chief Medical Examiner or another pathologist may conduct an autopsy upon request of the next-of kin. Reports of these autopsies requested only by next-of-kin are part of the decedent's medical records and are not public records open to inspection.

Health Assessments for Kindergarten Children in Public Schools - N.C. Gen. Stat. § 130A-441

Every child entering kindergarten in North Carolina public schools receives a medical health assessment. These health assessment files are open to inspection by the Department of Environment, Health and Natural Resources, the Department of Public Instruction, and their authorized representatives. People who inspect these files must maintain their confidentiality.

Farmworker Health Hazards - N.C. Gen. Stat. § 130A-460(a)

The Department of Environment, Health and Natural Resources and the Department of Labor exchange information about health hazards on farms. This information retains the same confidentiality provided by the originating agency.

Domiciliary Homes for People Who are Aged or Disabled - N.C. Gen. Stat. §§ 131D-2(b)(4), 131D-21(6), 131D-21.1, 131D-27, 131D-32(e)

The Department of Human Resources licenses, inspects and regulates domiciliary care homes for people who are aged or disabled.

Residents of domiciliary care homes have the right to have their personal and medical records kept confidential and not disclosed without written consent of the resident or his guardian. N.C. Gen. Stat. § 131D-21(6).

In the course of carrying out its regulatory duties, the Department may have access to confidential resident information. Confidential information and the names of people providing the information are exempt from the public records law. The Department may not disclose this confidential or privileged information without consent or a court order. N.C. Gen. Stat. § 131D-2(b)(4).

Under certain circumstances, resident medical records may be disclosed to private peer review committees approved by the Department. However, the peer review committee must keep these records confidential. N.C. Gen. Stat. § 131D-21.1

The Department may inspect residents' records at a facility to investigate complaints of alleged violations of residents' rights. The Department must maintain the confidentiality of all people who register these complaints with the Department and it must maintain the confidentiality of all records it inspects. N.C. Gen. Stat. § 131D-27.

Domiciliary home community advisory committees are authorized in counties with domiciliary homes. These committees resolve grievances between members of the community and these homes. The committees are required to keep the names of all people who file complaints and the names of residents involved in the complaint confidential unless written permission is given for disclosure. N.C. Gen. Stat. § 131D-32(e).

Lease or Sale of Public Hospitals to Corporations - N.C. Gen. Stat. § 131E-13(d)(5) and (8)

Municipalities and hospital authorities may sell, lease or convey a hospital to a corporation. Before doing so, they must give notice that copies of proposals for sale or lease are available to the public. Copies of proposed contracts for sale, lease or conveyance must be made available to the public at least ten days before the meeting at which the conveyance is approved.

Hospital Inspections - N.C. Gen. Stat. § 131E-80(d) and (e)

The Department of Human Resources licenses and inspects hospitals. In conducting these responsibilities, the Department may review written patient and employee records, including confidential and privileged information. Department employees may not disclose confidential or privileged information without authorization or a court order. Unauthorized disclosure is a criminal offense.

Other information obtained in these inspections or reports that is not privileged or confidential may be disclosed publicly, but no disclosure may icentify a patient without the patient's permission or a court order.

Hospital Medical Review Committees - N.C. Gen. Stat. § 131E-95

The proceedings of a medical review committee, the records and materials it produces and the materials it considers are confidential and are not public records.

In *Whisenhunt v. Zammit*, 86 N.C. App. 425, 358 S.E.2c 114 (1987), the North Carolina Court of Appeals held that a medical malpractice plaintiff could not require the production of a county hospital's credentialing file on the defendant doctor.

In *Cohn v. Wilkes General Hosp.*, 127 F.R.D. 117 (W.D.N.C. 1989), the U.S. District Court for the Western District of North Carolina ruled that a public hospital board's closed session consideration of physician credentialing information from a medical review committee was privileged and not subject to discovery.

Patient Information at Health Care Facilities - N.C. Gen. Stat. § 131E-97

Medical records, charges, accounts, credit histories, and other personal financial records compiled and kept by health care facilities in connection with the admission, treatment and discharge of individual patients are not public records.

Licensed chiropractors have access to their patients' diagnostic X-ray records and laboratory records at publicly supported hospitals. N.C. Gen. Stat. § 90-153; 48 N.C.A.G. 32 (1978).

Credentialing and Peer Review Information at Public Hospitals - N.C. Gen. Stat. § 131E-97.2

Information acquired by public hospitals, State-owned hospitals, and State-operated hospitals in connection with credentialing and peer review of people who have or seek privileges to practice in the hospital is confidential and is not a public record. However, information that is otherwise available to the public is not confidential merely because a hospital acquired it.

Competitive Health Care Information - N.C. Gen. Stat. § 131E-97.3

Information about competitive health care activities by or on behalf of hospitals is confidential and is not a public record. However, contracts entered into by or on behalf of public hospitals are public records unless otherwise exempted by law.

Hospital Patient Information Provided to the Department of Corrections - N.C. Gen. Stat. § 131E-98

A hospital does not breach patient confidentiality by providing the Department of Corrections with medical records of inmates who receive treatment at the hospital while in the custody of the Department of Corrections.

Inspections of Nursing Homes, Domiciliary Homes, Home Care Agencies, Ambulatory Surgical Facilities, Cardiac Rehabilitation Programs, Nursing Pools and Hospices - N.C. Gen. Stat. §§ 131E-105, 131E-117, 131E-141, 131E-150, 131E-154.8, 131E-170, and 131E-207

The Department of Human Resources licenses and inspects nursing homes, domiciliary homes, home care agencies, ambulatory surgical facilities, cardiac rehabilitation programs, nursing pools and hospices. Patient records at these facilities are confidential. In conducting its duties, the Department may review written patient records, including confidential and privileged information, unless the patient objects in writing. Patients must be given written notice that they may make objections to this disclosure of their records.[41] Department employees may not disclose confidential or privileged information without authorization or a court order. Department employees

---

In a 1981 opinion the North Carolina Attorney General said that it is insufficient for the Department to post a notice at facilities indicating that patients may object to this disclosure of their records. Patients should each be given a printed notice upon admission indicating their right to object to disclosure. 51 N.C.A.G. 17 (1981)

also may not disclose the name of any person who furnishes information about a facility unless that person consents. This confidential or privileged patient information, and the names of people furnishing information about facilities, are not public records.

Unauthorized disclosure of nursing pool and hospice information by Department employees is a criminal offense.

Peer Review Committees for Nursing Homes - N.C. Gen. Stat. § 131E-108

Under certain circumstances, medical records of nursing home residents may be disclosed to private peer review committees approved by the Department of Human Resources. However, the peer review committee must keep these records confidential.

Nursing Home Patient Bill of Rights - N.C. Gen. Stat. § 131E-117(5)

Personal and medical records of nursing home patients are confidential. The written consent of the patient must be obtained for release of these records to anyone, other than family members, except as needed in case of the patient's transfer to another health care institution or as required by law or a third party payment contract.

Nursing Home Complaint Investigations - N.C. Gen. Stat. § 131E-124

The Department of Human Resources investigates nursing home complaints. In doing so, the Department may inspect patient medical records. The Department is required to maintain the confidentiality of people who register complaints and the medical records it inspects.

Nursing Home Advisory Committees - N.C. Gen. Stat. § 131E-128(h)(4)

Nursing home community advisory committees are authorized in counties with nursing homes. These committees may investigate nursing home complaints and communicate with the Department of Human Resources about the interests of patients. The committees are required to keep the names of all people who file complaints confidential unless written permission is given for disclosure.

Certificates of Public Advantage for Hospital Cooperative Agreements - N.C. Gen. Stat. §§ 131E-192.7, 131E-192.9, and 131E-192.10

Hospitals may enter into cooperative agreements with other people or organizations without being subject to State antitrust laws if they get a certificate of public advantage from the Department of Human Resources.

The Department keeps on file all cooperative agreements for which certificates of public advantage are in effect. The Department also keeps on file notices that these agreements are terminated. These files are public records.

While certificates are in effect, reports of cooperative agreement activities must be filed every two years. The Department and the Attorney General may request additional information. Public comments may be filed after reports are filed. All reports, additional requested information, and public comments are public records.

Applicants or others who are aggrieved by a Department decision concerning a certificate of public advantage are entitled to judicial review of that decision. Also, the Department or the Attorney General may file suit to cancel a certificate. In any of these actions, the work product of the Department, the Attorney General or his staff is not a public record and is not discoverable or admissible.

North Carolina Medical Database Commission - N.C. Gen. Stat. §§ 131E-210, 131E-212(f) and 131E-213

The North Carolina Medical Database Commission collects and analyzes medical care cost and utilization data from health care providers and insurers. The individual forms, computer tapes, or other data collected by the Commission are not public records and are not subject to public inspection. The Commission must protect patient confidentiality (but it may make limited use of patient social security numbers to ensure the accuracy of its information base).[42] The Commission compiles aggregate data and makes this data available to people who are interested, including medical care providers, payors, consumers and planners.

Attorney-Client Communications - N.C. Gen. Stat. § 132-1.1(a)

The public records law says that certain written communications from attorneys to government bodies are not public records.

The following written communications from attorneys to government bodies, if they are made within the attorney-client privilege, are not public records:

(1) communications about claims against or on behalf of the government body;

(2) communications about claims against or on behalf of the governmental entity the government body represents;

(3) communications about the prosecution, defense, settlement or litigation of judicial actions, administrative proceedings, or other proceedings to which the government body is a party; and

---

In a 1987 opinion the North Carolina Attorney General confirmed that this limited use of patient social security numbers was consistent with federal law. 57 N.C.A.G. 38 (1987)

(4) communications about the prosecution, defense, settlement or litigation of judicial actions, administrative proceedings, or other proceedings which directly affect the government body, or which may directly affect the government body.

These kinds of written communications from attorneys are not subject to public inspection unless the government body that receives them decides to make them public.

Public inspection of these written communications from attorneys to government bodies is restricted in this way only for three years after the public body receives them. After that, these written communications automatically become public records and they are then subject to inspection by the public.

In *News & Observer Pub. Co. v. Poole*, 330 N.C. 465, 412 S.E.2d 7 (1992), the North Carolina Supreme Court issued important rulings on the scope of the attorney-client privilege for government agencies. The Court noted that although the public records law excepts written communications *from* attorneys *to* their public agencies, the law contains no exception for records of statements by members of a public agency to their attorney. The Court acknowledged that statements from nongovernmental clients to their attorneys are protected from disclosure by the traditional attorney-client privilege. However, the Court said that it had never recognized an attorney-client privilege for public entity clients, and it declined to decide whether this privilege extends to public entity clients in their communications to their attorneys. 330 N.C. at 482. To date, the public records law still only contains an exemption for written communications from government attorneys to their agencies. Whether written communications from agencies to their attorneys are exempt from disclosure has not been resolved by the courts or the General Assembly.

The Supreme Court in *Poole* also ruled that for attorney-to-agency communications to be exempt from disclosure, those communications must be in written form when they are made. In *Poole*, a government attorney, at a meeting of the agency he represented, gave verbal legal advice to the government agency he represented. The attorney's advice was recorded in the minutes of the agency's meeting. A newspaper sought disclosure of those minutes, and the agency claimed that they should not have to disclose those portions of the minutes containing the attorney's advice. The Supreme Court ruled that only those portions of minutes, which revealed *written* communications from the attorney were exempt from disclosure.

In a 1994 amendment to North Carolina's open meetings law, the General Assembly addressed one of the attorney-client issues disputed in *Poole*. The amendment states that the General Assembly acknowledges the existence of an attorney-client privilege between public bodies and their attorneys. N.C. Gen. Stat. § 143-318.11(a)(3). However, the amendment only clarifies the scope of the privilege in the context of attorney-client conversations held in closed sessions of meetings. This amendment says that public bodies do not have to disclose minutes of closed sessions in which they consult with their attorneys over legal matters, regardless of whether the communication is to or from the attorney.

However, the amendment does not address whether verbal attorney-agency conversations recorded in minutes of *open* sessions are subject to disclosure. Since minutes of open sessions are public records (N.C. Gen. Stat. § 143-318.10(e), presumably minutes of open sessions containing verbal attorney-agency conversations are public records. The amendment also does not expand the limited attorney-client privilege contained in the public records law, which still only applies to written communications *from* attorneys *to* the government agencies they represent.

Confidentiality of Tax Information - N.C. Gen. Stat. §§ 132-1.1(b), 105-259, 105-289(e), 153A-148.1 and 160A-208.1

The public records law says certain information from and about taxpayers may not be disclosed, except as allowed in North Carolina's tax laws.

The text of the public records law makes reference to the North Carolina tax laws, which restrict disclosure of tax information. These provisions are N.C. Gen. Stat. § 105-259 (disclosure by state employees and officials), §153A-148.1 (disclosure by county employees and officials), and § 160A-208.1 (disclosure by municipal employees and officials).

State employees and officials may not disclose any information about taxpayers' liability for taxes levied under authority of the state tax code (N.C. Gen. Stat. § 105, Subchapters I, V and VIII). Information that may not be disclosed includes:

(1) Information contained on a tax return,[43] a tax report, or an application for a license for which a tax is imposed;

(2) Information obtained in taxpayer audits or in taxpayer correspondence;

(3) Information about whether a taxpayer has filed a tax return or a tax report; and

(4) Lists of taxpayer names, addresses, social security numbers or similar taxpayer information.

In a 1973 opinion the North Carolina Attorney General said that the income tax returns of public school teachers were confidential and may not be disclosed by local boards of education. 42 N.C.A.G. 229 (1973)

State employees and officials are permitted to make limited disclosures of this information in 18 circumstances, which are listed in N.C. Gen. Stat. § 105-259(b). Many of these circumstances involve disclosure to other government agencies to assist them in carrying out various laws.

County and municipal employees and officials have access to this state tax information to assist them in levying local property taxes. These local employees and officials are also prohibited from disclosing this information publicly. N.C. Gen. Stat. § 105-296(h).

County and municipal employees and officials are prohibited from publicly disclosing local tax records that contain information about a taxpayer's income or receipts. N.C. Gen. Stat. § 153A-148.1 and § 160A-208.1. However, in a 1962 opinion the North Carolina Attorney General said that property tax listing abstracts are public records subject to public examination. 37 N.C.A.G. 85 (1962).

Disclosure in violation of these provisions is a criminal offense.

Trade Secrets - N.C. Gen. Stat. § 132-1.2

In the course of doing business with private companies, or in the course of regulating businesses, government agencies sometimes obtain trade secret information. The public records law states that it does not require or authorize public agencies to disclose trade secrets.

Trade secrets are defined by N.C. Gen. Stat. § 66-152(3). Trade secrets are business or technical information that has commercial value because it is not generally known or because it is not easily discoverable through independent development or reverse engineering. Trade secrets may include formulas, patterns, programs, devices, compilations of information, methods, techniques or processes. n order for information to be considered a trade secret, the efforts to maintain its secrecy must be reasonable under the circumstances.

For trade secret information to be exempt from disclosure by a public agency, the information must have been furnished to the agency through a business transaction with the agency (for example, performance of a contract or making of a bid, application or proposal), or the information must have been furnished to the agency in compliance with laws or regulations. Also, to keep trade secret information from being disclosed by a public agency the information should be designated or indicated as "confidential" or as a "trade secret" at the time the information is initially given to the agency.

In *North Carolina Elec. Membership Corp. v. North Carolina Dep't of Economic & Community Dev.*, 108 N.C. App. 711, 425 S.E.2d 440 (1993), the North Carolina Court of Appeals ruled that financial forecast documents and feasibility studies of an electric company submitted to State government in connection with a federal grant application were trade secrets, and were not subject to public inspection. Only one of these documents was actually designated as "confidential" when it was submitted to the government. However, the Court ruled that there was sufficient evidence that the company "indicated" the confidential nature of the other documents at the time of submission to the government for these other documents to be considered trade secrets.

In *S.E.T.A. UNC-CH, Inc. v. Huffines*, 101 N.C. App. 292, 399 S.E.2d 340 (1991), the North Carolina Court of Appeals ruled that information submitted to a State university review committee about the care and use of animals in proposed research experiments was not a trade secret and was subject to disclosure as public records. The court found that the information submitted was too general to be considered a trade secret.

Settlement Records - N.C. Gen. Stat. § 132-1.3

The public records law says that settlement documents in most lawsuits, administrative proceedings and arbitrations against public agencies are public records. Settlement documents are public records if the underlying suit or proceeding involves the public agency's official actions, duties or responsibilities. Settlement documents include settlement agreements, settlement correspondence, consent orders, documents dismissing or ending the proceeding, and payment documents such as checks or bank drafts.

A public agency may not enter into a settlement that includes a requirement that the settlement be kept confidential.

In some circumstances, judges or other people or panels presiding over the proceedings may order that settlement documents be sealed (not disclosed). Settlement documents may be sealed if the presumption of openness is overcome by an overriding interest, which cannot be protected by any measure short of sealing the settlement. If a settlement is sealed, the order sealing the settlement must state the overriding interest that is being protected by sealing the settlement. The order must also include specific findings of fact supporting the decision to seal the settlement, so that the decision may be reviewed by a higher court if necessary.

No settlement document that is sealed may be subject to public inspection.

This section of the public records law making settlement documents public records does not apply to settlements of medical malpractice actions against hospital facilities. Those settlement documents are not public records. Parties settling these actions may agree that the terms of the settlement are confidential.

Criminal Investigations and Criminal Intelligence Information - N.C. Gen. Stat. § 132-1.4

The public records law says that most criminal investigation records and criminal intelligence information compiled by public law enforcement agencies are not public records.

Criminal investigation records are those records or information compiled by law enforcement agencies when they are attempting to prevent or solve violations of criminal law. Criminal intelligence information is information compiled by law enforcement agencies in an effort to anticipate, prevent or monitor possible violations of criminal law.

Although most criminal investigation or intelligence information is not public, the public records law says that the following information is public:

(1) The time, date, location and nature of crimes or apparent crimes reported to law enforcement agencies;

(2) The name, sex, age, address, employment, and alleged crime of a person arrested, charged or indicted;

(3) The circumstances surrounding an arrest;

(4) The contents of "911" and other emergency calls, except the name, address, telephone number, or other information that identifies the caller, victim or witness;

(5) The contents of communications between law enforcement personnel that are broadcast over public airways;[44]

(6) The name, sex, age and address of a "complaining witness" (a crime victim or a person who reports a crime to a law enforcement agency.)

Even though this information is public, the public records law says that some of this information may be withheld from disclosure under certain circumstances.

A law enforcement agency is required to withhold temporarily the name and address of a complaining witness if releasing the information is likely to pose a threat to that person's mental health, physical health or personal safety. The agency is also required to withhold this information temporarily if releasing it might compromise a criminal investigation or intelligence operation. The law enforcement agency is required to release this information as soon as the reason for withholding it no longer exists.

Anyone seeking access to complaining witness information withheld by a law enforcement agency may seek a court order to require the release of the information.

Law enforcement agencies are not required to maintain tape recordings of "911" calls or other communications for more than 30 days after such calls are received, unless ordered to do so by a court. N.C. Gen. Stat. § 132-1.4(i).

Courts are required to give these requests priority over other cases. In deciding whether the information should be disclosed, the court should balance the interests of public disclosure against the interests of the complaining witness or law enforcement agency.

The other types of public criminal investigation and intelligence information listed above in items (1) through (5) may also be withheld by law enforcement agencies in some circumstances. Unlike information on complaining witnesses (item 6), however, the law enforcement agency must first get a court order before it may withhold this other information.

If a law enforcement agency wants to withhold these other listed items of public information, the agency must prove to the court that releasing the information will jeopardize the State's prosecution, jeopardize the defendant's right to a fair trial, or undermine an investigation.

Since some law enforcement records contain both nonpublic and public information, law enforcement agencies may release these records for inspection with the nonpublic information deleted. When law enforcement agencies provide copies of records with nonpublic information deleted, they are required to make it clear that a deletion has been made. They are also prohibited from destroying the original record.

If a law enforcement agency uses a document that is a public record to assist a criminal investigation or intelligence operation, the document remains a public record and is subject to disclosure requirements even though it is being used in a criminal investigation. For example, if a police department uses records of a person's prior convictions (which are public records) in a criminal investigation, the department may not withhold those records from public inspection.

Likewise, a law enforcement agency may not prevent another public agency from releasing public records simply because the law enforcement agency is using those records in a criminal investigation or intelligence operation. To use the example described above, a police department would not be able to prevent a court clerk from releasing criminal conviction records simply because those records were being used by the police in a criminal investigation.

The identities of confidential informants used by law enforcement agencies are not public records. Law enforcement agencies are not required to reveal information that is likely to identify confidential informants.

The North Carolina Criminal Procedure Act has several rules about what law enforcement investigation information the State must disclose to defendants prior to criminal trials. (See, generally, N.C. Gen. Stat. § 15A-901 through § 15A-910.) The public records law does not change these rules. The public records law says that records of criminal investigations and intelligence operations that are not required by the

Criminal Procedure Act to be disclosed to defendants are not required by the public records law to be disclosed to defendants or others.[45]

Similarly, the confidentiality or disclosure of child abuse investigation records are governed by N.C. Gen. Stat. § 7A-675, not by the public records law.

The following records in criminal cases are public records unless a court orders that they be sealed: arrest and search warrants that have been returned by law enforcement agencies, indictments, criminal summonses, and nontestimonial identification orders.

In a 1971 opinion, the North Carolina Attorney General said that police department arrest and disposition records are public records. 41 N.C.A.G. 407 (1971)

Business or Industrial Projects - N.C. Gen. Stat. §§ 132-6 and 132-9(b)

The public records law says that government records concerning the proposed expansion or location of specific businesses or industrial projects in the State are public records. However, these records may be withheld from public inspection temporarily if allowing inspection would frustrate the purpose for which the records were created. In general, this means that the agency with these records may withhold the records from public inspection if public knowledge of the records would interfere with negotiations or might deter a business from locating or expanding in the State. When the expansion or location is agreed upon or assured (in other words, when there is no longer a danger that releasing the records might prevent the project from materializing) the agency must then release the records for inspection.

The only public records that are subject to this temporary withholding are ones relating to specific business or industrial projects. Public records about general economic development policies and activities may not be withheld from public inspection.

If a public agency is sued to compel disclosure of records relating to business or industrial expansion projects, the agency has the burden of showing that disclosure would frustrate the purpose of attracting that particular business or industrial project. N.C. Gen. Stat. § 132-9(b).

This provision was added to the public records law in 1993 to ensure that the Act would not be used to obtain law enforcement information that defendants were not supposed to be able to get prior to their trials. A 1993 split decision of the North Carolina Supreme Court had reached the conclusion that the General Assembly did not intend for defendants to be able to obtain through the public records law what they could not obtain in criminal court discovery. *Piedmont Publishing Co., Inc. v. City of Winston-Salem*, 334 N.C. 595, 434 S.E.2d 176 (1993). The 1993 amendment to the public records law confirmed and codified this conclusion.

Geographical Information Systems - N.C. Gen. Stat. § 132-10

Geographical information systems databases and data files developed and operated by counties and cities are public records. Counties and cities must provide access to these systems by public access terminals or other output devices. Upon request, counties and cities must provide copies of these databases in documentary or electronic form to anyone at a reasonable cost. However, as a condition of furnishing electronic copies counties and cities may require written agreement from people receiving copies that they will not redistribute the copies for trade or commercial purposes. Publication and broadcast by news media is not considered resale or distribution for trade or commercial purposes. Also, use of information without resale by a licensed professional in the course of practicing his profession is not considered use for a commercial purpose.

Public Contract Bidding - N.C. Gen. Stat. § 133-33

State and local government agencies that make public contracts may adopt rules about the confidentiality of: 1) the agency's cost estimate for any public contracts prior to bidding; and 2) the identity of contractors who have obtained proposals for bid purposes for a public contract.

Agencies that make these items confidential may discipline employees or officers who make unauthorized disclosures of this information.

Rules of Commission of Youth Services - N.C. Gen. Stat. § 134A

The Division of Youth Services in the Department of Human Resources runs training schools for committed delinquents. The Commission of Youth Services, which oversees the Division, adopts rules related to the supervision and rights of youths under its supervision or in its custody. These rules are published by the Attorney General's Office and are made available for public inspection by the Commission.

Teachers' and State Employees' Retirement System - N.C. Gen. Stat. § 135-6(i) and (p)

The Board of Trustees of the Teachers' and State Employees' Retirement System keeps a record of all its proceedings. This record is open to public inspection. The Board also publishes annually a report showing the fiscal transactions of the Retirement System for the preceding year, the amount of the accumulated cash and securities of the System, and the last balance sheet showing the financial condition of the System.

Government agencies participating in the Retirement System may provide to the System the social security numbers, names and addresses of members and beneficiaries. This information may be used only to inform members and beneficiaries about benefits, and is otherwise confidential. Unauthorized disclosure of this information is a criminal offense.

Teachers' and State Employees' Comprehensive Major Medical Plan - N.C. Gen. Stat. § 135-37

All information about participants in the Teachers' and State Employees' Comprehensive Major Medical Plan which is in the possession of the Plan's administrator and board is confidential and is not subject to disclosure under the public records law.

Highway Construction Bids - N.C. Gen. Stat. § 136-28.1(b)

When the Department of Transportation lets contracts for highway construction or repair for $300,000.00 or less, it does so by soliciting at least three informal bids. A record of all bids received is kept by the Transportation Secretary, and this record is available for public inspection at any time after the bids are opened.

Highway Construction - Construction Diaries and Bid Analyses - N.C. Gen. Stat. § 136-28.5

Diaries kept in connection with construction and repair contracts entered into with the Department of Transportation are not public records until the final estimate has been paid.

Analyses generated by the Department of Transportation's Bid Analysis and Management System are confidential and are not public records.

Test Drilling or Boring on Roads under Department of Transportation Jurisdiction - N.C. Gen. Stat. § 136-102.2

Test drilling or boring on a right-of-way, road or highway under the jurisdiction of the Department of Transportation may not be done without written permission of the landowner or person in charge of the land. A complete record of the results of the test must be filed with the Department, and it is a public record.

Test Drilling or Boring on Public Land - N.C. Gen. Stat. § 136-102.3

The results of test drilling or boring on any public land owned or controlled by the State of North Carolina must be filed with the Secretaries of Administration and Environment, Health and Natural Resources. These are public records.

Organizations Receiving State Funds - N.C. Gen. Stat. § 143-6 1

Corporations and organizations receiving or spending $25,000 or more in State funds annually must file financial statements with the State Auditor and the Joint Legislative Commission on Governmental Operations. These statements, along with all reports or audits produced as a result of this information, are public records.

Joint Meetings of Legislative Budget Committees - N.C. Gen. Stat. § 143-14

The appropriations committees of the North Carolina House of Representatives and Senate are to sit jointly in open session while considering the budget.

Bids for State Government Supplies, Materials, Contractual Services and Equipment - N.C. Gen. Stat. §§ 143-52 and 143-53(9)

Bids to provide State government supplies, materials, contractual services and equipment are, after the award of the contract, open to public inspection. However, trade secrets, test data and similar proprietary information may remain confidential. The Secretary of Administration may adopt rules on the conditions under which this information may remain confidential.

Certain Public Hospital Equipment and Supply Purchases are Excepted from Government Contracting Procedures - N.C. Gen. Stat. § 143-129(f)

Most large purchases ($20,000 or more) of equipment, supplies or services, and large construction or repair contracts ($50,000 or more) by State and local governments must be done in accordance with bidding and contracting procedures. However, the purchase of some specialized equipment and supplies by public hospitals may be done without following these procedures. Hospitals keep records of equipment and supplies purchased without normal bidding and contracting procedures. These records are subject to public inspection.

Local Government Small Contracts - N.C. Gen. Stat. § 143-131

Local government contracts for construction, repair or purchases, in amounts over $5000 (but less than $50,000 for construction and less than $20,000 for purchases) are done in accordance with informal bidding procedures. Agencies entering into contracts after bidding keep records of all bids submitted. These records are open to public inspection at any time.

Construction and Repair Work Done by State or Local Employees - N.C. Gen. Stat. § 143-135

Public construction or repair work done by State or local employees for $75,000 or less need not be done in accordance with bidding and contracting procedures. However, State and local agencies are required to keep complete and accurate records of the work done, and these records are available for inspection by the general public.

Building Code Council - N.C. Gen. Stat. § 143-137

All meetings of the Building Code Council are open to the public.

Sewage Pretreatment Program Applications - N.C. Gen. Stat. § 143-215.1(d)(1)

Local government units who grant permits for sewage pretreatment facilities keep lists of pretreatment applications received. These lists are available to the public upon request.

Environmental Management Commission Investigation Records - N.C. Gen. Stat. § 143-215.3C

Records, reports or information obtained by the Environmental Management Commission as part of its investigatory authority under North Carolina's Water and Air Resources law, Oil Pollution and Hazardous Substances Control Act, and Air Pollution Control law (Articles 21, 21A and 21B of Chapter 143 of the General Statutes) are available to the public, unless making them public would divulge trade secrets. Effluent data are not entitled to confidential treatment. Those objecting to the Commission's decision on whether certain information should be confidential or should be released are entitled to request a declaratory ruling. Information subject to these requests may not be released until the ruling is issued, or until a final judicial determination is made.

Water Capacity Use Areas - N.C. Gen. Stat. § 143-215.19(e)

The Environmental Management Commission designates areas in the State where it regulates the use of water sources. In doing so, the Commission may inspect water use facilities and request information about water use. When the Commission demands or requests this information, it must indicate that trade secrets or confidential business information is entitled to confidential treatment. The Commission keeps this information confidential.

Dam Safety Law - N.C. Gen. Stat. § 143-215.37

The Environmental Management Commission regulates and inspects dams. The Commission may require written statements about the construction or operation of a dam. However, no one is required to disclose any secret formulas, processes or methods used in any manufacturing operation or any confidential information about business activities.

Water and Air Pollution Reports - N.C. Gen. Stat. § 143-215.65

Those who discharge waste into water, and those who emit air contaminants, are required to file reports on these emissions to the Environmental Management Commission. The Commission uses this information only for the purpose of air and water pollution control. The Commission is required to preserve the confidentiality of proprietary manufacturing processes, but this confidentiality does not extend to information about wastes discharged or air contaminants emitted.

Oil Pollution and Hazardous Substances Control Act - N.C. Gen. Stat. § 143-215.80

The Environmental Management Commission regulates and investigates the storage and disposal of hazardous substances. Trade secret information discovered or obtained by the Commission in carrying out these duties may not be revealed except as required by law or legal orders.

Public Hospital Boards - N.C. Gen. Stat. § 143-318.10(b)

The open meetings law specifies that certain boards associated with public hospitals are public bodies subject to the law. A board is a public body if it is the governing board of:

1) a public hospital[46];

2) a nonprofit corporation to which a publicly owned hospital facility has been sold or conveyed;

3) any subsidiary of such nonprofit corporation; and

4) any nonprofit corporation owning the corporation to which a publicly owned hospital facility has been sold or conveyed.

Government Bodies Not Subject to the Open Meetings Law - N.C. Gen. Stat. § 143-318.10(c) and § 143-318.18

The open meetings law specifies that it does not apply to the following government bodies:

1) Grand and petit juries;

2) Any public body authorized by law to meet in closed session, to the extent they are authorized to meet in closed session;

3) The Judicial Standards Commission;

4) The Legislative Ethics Committee;

5) A conference committee of the General Assembly;

In *Cohn v. Wilkes General Hosp.*, 127 F.R.D. 117 (W.D.N.C. 1989), the U.S. District Court for the Western District of North Carolina ruled that Wilkes General Hospital was a public hospital, whose closed session discussions about the rejection of medical staff privileges were privileged and not subject to discovery.

6) A caucus by members of the General Assembly. However, no member of the General Assembly may take part in a caucus, which is called to evade or subvert the open meetings law;

7) Law enforcement agencies;

8) Professional and occupational licensing boards that determine applicant qualifications and take disciplinary actions are not subject to the open meetings law when: i) they are preparing, approving, administering, or grading examinations; or ii) they are meeting with respect to applicants or licensees;

9) Public bodies that are subject to the Executive Budget Act, Chapter 143 of the General Statutes (most state government administrative agencies) are not subject to the open meetings law when they meet to make decisions in adjudicatory actions;

10) Boards of trustees of endowment funds authorized by Chapters 116-36 and 116-238 of the General Statutes;

11) The Board of Awards; and

12) The General Court of Justice.[47]

N.C. Gen. Stat. § 143-318.18

The open meetings law also says that the following are not public bodies subject to the law:

1. A meeting solely among the professional staff of a public body; or

2. The medical staff of a public hospital.

N.C. Gen. Stat. § 143-318.10(c)

In *News & Observer Pub. Co. v. Poole*, 330 N.C. 465, 412 S.E.2d 7 (1992), The North Carolina Supreme Court ruled that government agencies which are not "public bodies" pursuant to the open meetings law, are not automatically exempted from the disclosure requirements of the public records law.

In *Poole*, a governmental investigative commission did not fall within the

---

Although the courts are not subject to the open meetings law, Article I, Section 18 of the North Carolina Constitution requires in general that all courts shall be open. Certain types of hearings such as juvenile proceedings are closed to the public, however.

definition of a "public body" in the open meetings law. A newspaper sought records of the commission, including minutes of its meetings and drafts of its final reports. The commission argued that since it was not subject to the open meetings law, it did not have to disclose its records pursuant to the public records law.

The Court disagreed with the commission. The Court indicated that the definition of a "public body" under the open meetings law was narrower than the definition of a "public agency" under the public records law. The Court said the public records law and the open meetings law are discrete statutes, each designed to promote openness in government in a different way. The Court said there is no suggestion in either statute that an agency not subject to one is automatically exempt from the other.

Legislative Commissions, Committees and Standing Subcommittees - N.C. Gen. Stat. § 143-318.14A

All official meetings of commissions, committees, standing subcommittees, standing subcommittees and study committees of the General Assembly must be held in open session. (As discussed above in *Government Bodies Not Subject to the Open Meetings Law,* the Legislative Ethics Committee, General Assembly caucuses and conference committees are not subject to the open meetings law. N.C. Gen. Stat. § 143-318.18)

Reasonable public notice must be given for these meetings. Reasonable public notice includes giving notice openly at a session of the Senate or House, or posting notice on the pressroom door of the Legislative Building and delivering notice to the Legislative Services Office.

Violating these provisions is punishable according to the rules of the Senate and House.

Meetings of these commissions and committees are subject to the open meetings law provisions on minutes, closed sessions, electronic meetings, written ballots, acting by reference, broadcasting, recording, civil actions and disruptions of meetings.

Environmental Management Commission Legislative Proposals - N.C. Gen. Stat. § 143-354(a)(7)

All recommendations for proposed legislation made by the Environmental Management Commission are available to the public.

Department of Environment, Health and Natural Resources Records Climatological and Water-Resources Records - N.C. Gen. Stat. § 143-355(b)(12)

The Department of Environment, Health and Natural Resources prepares and keeps climatological and water resources records and files as a source of information easily accessible to the public.

Vocational Rehabilitation Advisory Council Annual Report - N.C. Gen. Stat. § 143-548(d3) and (4)

The Vocational Rehabilitation Advisory Council publishes an annual report, which is available to the public.

Repayment of Money Owed by Employees and Officials of the State and of Boards of Education and Boards of Community Colleges - N.C. Gen. Stat. § 143-560

State law requires that certain employees and officials of the State, boards of education, and boards of community colleges repay money owed to the State. Otherwise confidential information about these individuals may be exchanged by their employing agencies to carry out the purposes of this law.

North Carolina Child Fatality Prevention System - N.C. Gen. Stat. § 143-578

The North Carolina Child Fatality Task Force, the North Carolina Child Fatality Prevention Team and the local Community Child Protection Teams collect information and work toward preventing the abuse and neglect of children and child deaths.

These agencies have access to police investigation records, child protective services records and health data, which are confidential. Members and employees of these agencies may not reveal this confidential information.

Meetings of the State Team and Local Teams are rot subject to the open meetings law. Local teams may hold public meetings to discuss, in a general manner not revealing confidential information about children and families, the findings of their reviews and their recommendations for preventive actions. Minutes of all public meetings, excluding those of closed sessions, are kept in compliance with the open meetings law. Any minutes or other information generated during a closed session are sealed from public inspection.

State Health Plan Purchasing Alliance Board - N.C. Gen. Stat. § 143-625(h)

Meetings of the State Health Plan Purchasing Alliance Board are governed by the open meetings law.

State Health Plan Purchasing Alliances - N.C. Gen. Stat. § 143-627(i)

Meetings of the boards of State Health Plan Purchasing Alliances are governed by the open meetings law.

Medical Records in Possession of Department of Human Resources - N.C. Gen. Stat. § 143B-139.6

All privileged patient medical records in the possession of the Department of Human Resources are confidential and are not public records.

Commission for the Blind Annual Report - N.C. Gen. Stat. § 143B-157(3d)

The Commission for the Blind prepares an annual report, which is available to the public.

North Carolina Partnership for Children, Inc. - N.C. Gen. Stat. § 143B-168.12(a) and § 143B-168.14(a)(2)

As a condition for receiving funding, the North Carolina Partnership for Children, Inc. must adopt operational procedures comparable to the open meetings law and the public records law.

Early childhood initiatives local partnerships must also adopt operational procedures comparable to the open meetings law and the public records law.

Complaints to State/Regional Long-Term Care Ombudsmen - N.C. Gen. Stat. §§ 143B-181.18 and 143B-181.22

State and Regional Long-Term Care Ombudsmen investigate and attempt to resolve complaints concerning long-term care facilities. The identities of complainants, residents on whose behalf complaints are made, or people who provide information in investigations or complaints are confidential and may be disclosed only with express permission of these people.

Department of Correction Rules - N.C. Gen. Stat. § 143B-261.1

The Department of Correction's rules related to the conduct, supervision, rights and privileges of people in its custody and under its supervision are available for public inspection.

Deliberations of the Environmental Management Commission - N.C. Gen. Stat. § 143B-282.1

The Environmental Management Commission has quasi-judicial powers in contested cases under a variety of environmental statutes. The Commission's deliberations are conducted in public meetings unless it determines that consultation with its attorney should be held in closed session pursuant to the open meetings law.

Minutes of Board of Transportation Meetings - N.C. Gen. Stat. § 143B-350(e)

The minutes of the meetings of the Board of Transportation are at all times open to public inspection.

Governor's Advocacy Council for Persons with Disabilities - N.C. Gen. Stat. § 143B-403.1(1)

The Governor's Advocacy Council for Persons with Disabilities investigates complaints by or on behalf of people residing in facilities for the mentally or developmentally disabled. The Council is required to keep client information confidential in accordance with federal laws.

Economic Development Board Annual Reports - N.C. Gen. Stat. § 143B-434.01(l)

The Economic Development Board makes public reports available annually on the progress toward attaining the objectives of the Comprehensive Strategic Economic Development Plan.

Energy Division of Department of Commerce - Information on Petroleum Supplies - N.C. Gen. Stat. § 143B-450.1(f)

During current or impending energy crises, the Energy Division of the Department of Commerce may obtain information from prime petroleum suppliers about supplies of petroleum products. The Division is required to keep confidential any information identifying people and other sources of information.

Meetings of North Carolina Mutual Burial Association Commission - N.C. Gen. Stat. § 143B-472.2

All regular and special meetings of the North Carolina Mutual Burial Association Commission are open to the public, unless a majority of the members of the Commission vote otherwise. All regular meetings are to be advertised in at least three newspapers with intercounty circulation in North Carolina.

North Carolina Center for Missing Persons - N.C. Gen. Stat. §§ 143B-498(2) and 143B-499.6

The North Carolina Center for Missing Persons in the Department of Crime Control and Public Safety collects and disseminates information on missing persons to authorized law enforcement agencies. It is a criminal offense for anyone working with the Center to make an unauthorized release of this information.

State Auditor Work Papers - N.C. Gen. Stat. § 147-64.6(d)

Audit work papers of the State Auditor are confidential, unless they are subpoenaed by a court or court official, or unless the Auditor makes them available to other State or federal agencies who desire access and inspection of them in connection with some matter officially before them.

State Auditor Investigations Referred to the General Assembly - N.C. Gen. Stat. § 147-64.12(b)

If the Auditor receives a report of allegations of improper governmental activities, which he is not permitted to audit because of a conflict of interest, he is to refer the report to the Legislative Administrative Officer. The report retains the same confidentiality in the General Assembly that it had in the possession of the Auditor.

State Treasurer Quarterly Financial Reports - N.C. Gen. Stat. § 147-69.1(e)

The State Treasurer prepares a quarterly report of the State's cash, deposits and investments. This report is posted in the Treasurer's office for the information of the public.

Department of Correction Responses to Inmate Grievances - N.C. Gen. Stat. § 148-118.5

All reports, investigations and supporting documents prepared by the Department of Correction in response to prisoners' requests for administrative remedies are confidential. All formal written responses to prisoners' requests are furnished to the prisoners.

The Grievance Resolution Board has access to all relevant records developed by the Department of Corrections.

Transfers of Prisoners to Other States - Public Comment - N.C. Gen. Stat. § 148-121(b) and (c)

Before transferring a North Carolina prisoner to another state, the Secretary of Correction gives public notice and an opportunity to submit comments. Written comments on prisoner transfers are public records, unless the Secretary determines that disclosure would jeopardize the safety of people or property.

Contested Case Administrative Hearings - N.C. Gen. Stat. §§ 150B-23(e) and 150B-38(e)

Administrative hearings of contested cases held before administrative law judges and administrative agencies are open to the public.

Township Boundaries - N.C. Gen. Stat. § 153A-19

The current boundaries of all townships within each county are drawn on a map or set out in a written description, which are available for public inspection in the office of the clerk of each board of county commissioners.

Regular and Special Meetings of Boards of County Commissioners - N.C. Gen. Stat. § 153A-40

Each county board of commissioners is required to hold at least one regular meeting each month, but it may hold more regular meetings if t wishes to. The board may adopt a resolution fixing a time and place for regular meetings. If they do so, they must post a copy of the resolution on the courthouse door at least 10 days before the first regular meeting, and they must also publish a summary of the resolution. If the board does not fix a time and place for regular meetings, it must meet at the courthouse on the first Monday of each month (or on the next business day if the first Monday is a holiday).

The board may temporarily change the time or place of a regular meeting or all regular meetings within a specified time. The board must post a notice of this change at the courthouse or its regular meeting place, and it should take other helpful action to inform the public of the temporary change.

The board may adjourn a regular meeting from one day to the next, or until a specified day, until the business before the board is completed.[48]

The chairman or a majority of the board may call special board meetings. They may do so by signing a notice of the time and place of the meeting and the subjects to be considered at the meeting. Whoever calls the special meeting must deliver the notice to the chairman and all board members at least 48 hours before the meeting, and must post a copy of the notice on the courthouse bulletin board at least 48 hours before the meeting. At a special meeting, only those items of business specified in the notice may be transacted, unless all members are present or those not present have signed a written waiver.

If a special meeting is called to deal with an emergency, the notice requirements for special meetings do not apply. However, the person calling the meeting is required to take reasonable action to inform the other board members and the public of the meeting. At emergency meetings, only business connected with the emergency may be

---

In *Wright v. County of Macon*, 64 N.C. App. 718, 308 S.E.2d 97 (1983), the North Carolina Court of Appeals ruled that a county board of commissioners complied with N.C. Gen. Stat. § 153A-40 by adjourning a regular meeting on August 2 and posting notice on August 13 that the meeting would be reconvened on August 16.

discussed.

A person calling a special or emergency meeting must also comply with the notice requirements of the open meetings law, N.C. Gen. Stat. § 143-318.12.

With a few exceptions, boards of commissioners must hold their meetings in their own county. Boards may meet out of the county at joint meetings with other public bodies, but these meetings must be held in the jurisdiction of one of the public bodies. Boards may hold retreats out of their counties, but they may not vote or transact business while there. Boards may meet out of the county with their local legislative delegation during a session of the General Assembly, but they may not vote or transact business while there. Board members may meet out of the county at conventions, association meetings, and similar gatherings. However, they may meet there only to discuss and deliberate on convention or association resolutions and elections.

Board meetings held outside the county are official meetings under the open meetings law.

Minutes of Proceedings of County Boards of Commissioners and Municipal Councils - N.C. Gen. Stat. §§ 153A-42 and 160A-72

The minutes of the proceedings of county boards of commissioners and municipal councils are kept and made available for public inspection by county or municipal clerks.

Technical Ordinances Adopted by Reference into County and Municipal Ordinances - N.C. Gen. Stat. §§ 153A-47 and 160A-76(b)

A county or municipality may in an ordinance adopt by reference a published technical code or a standard or regulation promulgated by a public agency. An official copy of a technical code, standard or regulation adopted by reference is to be kept available for public inspection in the county or municipal clerk's office.

County and Municipal Ordinance Books - N.C. Gen. Stat. §§ 153A-48 and 160A-78

County and municipal clerks keep ordinance books separate from minute books. Ordinance books are available for inspection in clerks' offices.

Public Hearings Before County Boards of Commissioners and City Councils - N.C. Gen. Stat. §§ 153A-52 and 160A-81

County boards of commissioners and municipal councils may hold public hearings at any place within their jurisdictions. Boards and councils may adopt reasonable rules for conducting these hearings, including:

(1)   time allotted for each speaker;

(2) designating spokesmen for groups of people supporting or opposing the same position;

(3) selecting delegates from groups of people with similar positions when the number of people who want to attend the hearing exceeds the capacity of the hearing room; and

(4) providing for the maintenance of order and decorum in the hearing.

Public hearings may be continued without further advertisement. If a public hearing is set for a given date and a quorum of the board is not present, the board may continue the hearing without further advertisement until its next regular meeting.

In *Leak v. High Point City Council*, 25 N.C. App. 394, 213 S.E.2d 386 (1975), the North Carolina Court of Appeals ruled that there was no justification for excluding live radio and television coverage of city council investigative hearings on police corruption.

County and Municipal Managers' Annual Reports - N.C. Gen. Stat. §§ 153A-82(6) and 160A-148(6)

County and municipal managers submit annual reports to their boards and councils on their counties' and municipalities' finances and administrative activities. These reports are available to the public.

Special Assessments by Counties and Municipalities - N.C. Gen. Stat. §§ 153A-194 and 160A-227

Counties and municipalities may pay for certain improvements by assessing benefited property for all or part of the costs of the projects.

The county board or municipal council prepares a preliminary assessment roll indicating properties to be assessed, the basis for assessments, and the amounts to be assessed. The board or council holds a hearing on the proposal. Before the hearing, the preliminary assessment roll is available for public inspection in the county or municipal clerk's office.

Jail Inspections - N.C. Gen. Stat. § 153A-222

The Department of Human Resources inspects local jails and detention centers. In doing so, Department officials may have access to confidential medical information of patients and residents, if the patients or residents do not object. Patients must be given written notice that they may object to disclosure of their records.[49] This information is

---

In a 1981 opinion the North Carolina Attorney General said that it is insufficient for the Department to post a notice at facilities indicating that patients may object to this disclosure of their records. Patients should each be given a printed notice upon admission indicating their right to object to disclosure. 51 N.C.A.G. 17 (1981)

not a public record. Department officials are not permitted to disclose this confidential information unless they have the consent of the person or his legal representative, or unless they are ordered to disclose the information by a court.

The Department is also not permitted to disclose the name of any person who furnishes information about a facility. Names of people who furnish this information are not public records.

County, Municipal, and Urban Service Districts - N.C. Gen. Stat. §§ 153A-302(b), 153A-303(d), 153A-304((b), 153A-312(c), 153A-314(b), 160A-537(b) and (e), 160A-538(c), 160A-539(b), 160B-6(b), 160B-7(c), and 160B-8(b)

Counties, municipalities and consolidated city-counties may establish service districts for such things as fire protection, ambulance services, recreation, research and production, water supply, and waste disposal. County boards and municipal councils must hold public hearings before establishing, extending or consolidating service districts. Before holding a hearing, the board or council must publish a report describing and justifying the proposed action regarding a service district. This report is available for public inspection in the county or municipal clerk's office before the public hearing.

Regional Planning Commissions - N.C. Gen. Stat. §§ 153A-394 and 153A-397

All meetings of regional planning commissions are open to the public.

Regional planning commissions prepare annual reports to distribute to their member governments. These reports are available to the public.

Regional Solid Waste Management Authorities - N.C. Gen. Stat. § 153A-425

All meetings of regional solid waste management authorities are subject to the open meetings law.

Public Housing Authority Hearings - N.C. Gen. Stat. § 157-9

Public housing authorities may hold public or private hearings on matters that are material for their information.

Local Government Budgets - N.C. Gen. Stat. §§ 159-12(a) and 159-17

Proposed budgets of local governments are available for public inspection before adoption.

Local government governing boards may call special meetings to complete their work on budget ordinances. The notice requirements of the open meetings law apply to these meetings.

In a 1973 opinion the North Carolina Attorney General said that municipal books and papers, such as budgets, bank statements, tax levies, utility accounts and minutes of meetings are all public records which may be inspected by members of the public. 43 N.C.A.G. 274 (1973).

Local Government Bond Orders - N.C. Gen. Stat. § 159-54(5)

Before issuing bonds, local governments must introduce bond orders. Bond orders must state, among other things, that a sworn statement of debt has been filed with the clerk and is open to public inspection.

Joint Municipal Electric Agencies - N.C. Gen. Stat. § 159B-38

Records on discussions of the following contracts or proposed contracts of joint municipal electric agencies are confidential and are not public records:

(1) contracts for the construction, ownership, or operation of works, plants, and facilities for or incident to the generation, transmission, or use of electric power and energy; and

(2) contracts for the purchase, sale, exchange, interchange, wheeling, pooling, transmission, or use of electric power or energy.

However, contracts entered into by or on behalf of joint agencies are public records unless otherwise exempted by law.

Ownership of Registered Public Obligations - N.C. Gen. Stat. § 159E-11(a)

Records indicating the ownership of or security interests in registered public obligations are not subject to inspection or copying as public records. However, records of a public entity's own holdings in registered public obligations are subject to inspection and copying as public records.

Municipal Annexation - N.C. Gen. Stat. § 160A-49(b) and (c)

A municipal board, which is planning to annex territory to the municipality, must prepare a report describing and justifying the annexation plan. This report is available for public inspection before the public hearing at which the annexation is considered.

Regular and Special Meetings of City and Town Councils - N.C. Gen. Stat. § 160A-71

City and town councils must fix the time and place for their regular meetings. If they do not do so, they are required to hold a regular meeting at least once a month at 10:00 a.m. on the first Monday of the month.

The mayor, the mayor pro tempore, or any two members of the council may call a special council meeting at any time. They may do so by signing a written notice stating the time and place of the special meeting and the subject to be considered. The notice must be delivered to the mayor and each council member at least six hours before the meeting. At a special meeting, only those items of business specified in the notice may be transacted, unless all members are present or unless they have signed a written waiver of notice. A person who calls a special meeting must also comply with the meeting notice requirements of the open meetings law, N.C. Gen. Stat. § 143-318.12.

The council may, during any regular meeting, call or schedule a special meeting. They must do so by motion or resolution, adopted in an open session, specifying the time, place and purpose of the special meeting.

Any regular or special meeting may be recessed or adjourned by the council to reconvene at a specified time and place.

A council may adopt its own rules of procedure, which must be consistent with the city charter, general law, and generally accepted principles of parliamentary procedure.

City and Town Council Minutes - N.C. Gen. Stat. § 160A-72

Minutes of city and town council proceedings are open to the inspection of the public.

Procedures for Claims Against Local Government Officials and Employees - N.C. Gen. Stat. § 160A-167(c)

Local governments may defend civil and criminal claims against their current or former governing board members, officials, and employees. Before a local government pays a claim or judgment against any of these people, it must have adopted and made available for public inspection uniform standards under which claims are made or civil judgments are entered.

Local Preservation Commission Meetings - N.C. Gen. Stat. §§ 160A-440.6(4) and 160A-400.9(c)

All meetings of local preservation commissions are open to the public in accordance with the open meetings law.

Meetings and Annual Reports of Regional Councils of Government - N.C. Gen. Stat. §§ 160A-473 and 160A-477

All meetings of regional councils of governments are open to the public.

Regional councils prepare annual reports, which they distribute to their member governments and the public.

Meetings of Regional Sports Authorities - N.C. Gen. Stat. § 160A-479.5

All meetings of regional sports authorities are open to the public.

Redevelopment Commissions - N.C. Gen. Stat. §§ 160A-512(9), 160A-513(h), and 160A-521

Redevelopment commissions may hold public or private hearings on any matter material for their information.

Before a redevelopment plan is acted upon, there must be a public hearing. Before a hearing, the redevelopment plan must be available for public inspection at a place designated in the hearing notice.

The books and records of redevelopment commissions are open and subject to public inspection at all times. Copies of redevelopment commission bylaws, rules and regulations are filed with city clerks and are open for public inspection.

Metropolitan Water District Financial Reports - N.C. Gen. Stat. § 162A-36(b)(1)

Metropolitan water districts are required to publish annual financial reports, and their books are open for public inspection.

Extension of Water and Sewer Districts - N.C. Gen. Stat. § 162A-87.1(d)

Before extending water and sewer districts, counties must hold public hearings. Before holding a hearing, the county board must publish a report describing and justifying the proposed extension. This report is available for public inspection in the board clerk's office for at least two weeks prior to the public hearing.

Voter Registration Records - N.C. Gen. Stat. §§ 163-82.4(b), 163-82.10(b) and (c), 163-82.13, 163-82.20(f), 163-84

People may register to vote at county boards of elections and certain other State agencies. Voter registration forms must include a statement that if the applicant declines to register to vote, that fact will remain confidential and will be used for voter registration only. Registration forms must also state that if an applicant does register to vote, the office at which the applicant submits a voter registration application will remain confidential and will be used only for voter registration purposes.

Information relating to a declination to register to vote in connection with an application made at a voter registration agency may not be used for any purpose other than voter registration.

County boards of elections must furnish a list of all registered voters in the county to any person upon request and reimbursement for the actual cost of preparing the list. State and county party chairs are entitled to receive these lists for free on a periodic basis.

County boards of elections may upon request supply selective lists of voters according to party affiliation, sex, race, date of registration, or other reasonable category.

The voter registration records of each county are open to inspection by any registered voter of the county at the county board of elections office during regular business hours.

The State Board of Elections must make available to the chair of each political party one free magnetic copy of the statewide computerized voter registration file after the close of registration before each statewide primary and election. These statewide voter registration records are to be made available for sale to other people and organizations beginning January 1, 1996.

The State Board of Elections may sell selective lists of registered voters according to county, congressional or legislative district, party affiliation, gender, date of birth, race, date of registration, or other categories.

Election Precinct Maps - N.C. Gen. Stat. § 163-128(b)

County boards of elections prepare and revise maps of election precinct boundaries. These maps are posted for public inspection at board offices.

Ballot Counting - N.C. Gen. Stat. §§ 163-169(c) and (e), 163-171.

The counting of ballots in precincts is to be done in the presence of the precinct election officials and witnesses and observers who are present and desire to observe the count. Observers are not to interfere with the counting.

In primary elections ballots are emptied on a table in full view of precinct officials, ballot counters and witnesses. Results of ballot counts are to be read aloud.

On the night of a primary or election, unofficial and official precinct reports of voting are reported to county boards of elections. The county board of elections must publish these reports to the press, radio, and television.

When the precinct count of ballots is completed after a primary or election, all ballots are put back in ballot boxes, which are locked and sealed. Ballot boxes may be opened only upon an order from the county board of elections or a court. Ballots are kept for at least two months after the primary or election.

Registers of Absentee Ballots - N.C. Gen. Stat. §§ 163-228 and 163-248

Each county board of elections keeps a register of absentee ballot applications and ballots issued. This register is open to the inspection of any registered voter of the county at any time within 50 days before and 30 days after an election in which absentee ballots are authorized, or at any other time when good and sufficient reason may be assigned for its inspection.

Each county board of elections also keeps a register of military absentee ballot applications and ballots issued. This register is open to any registered voter of the county at any time.

Authorizations for Media Advertising in Elections - N.C. Gen. Stat. § 163-278.17

Before electoral candidates may spend money to make political advertisements in media, each media organization is required to get written authority for each expenditure from each candidate, campaign treasurer or individual making or authorizing an expenditure. All these written authorizations are public records. Copies of these authorizations are available for inspection during normal business hours at the media offices nearest to the place of publication or broadcast.

State Board of Elections - N.C. Gen. Stat. § 163-279.22(4)

It is the duty of the State Board of Elections to make statements and other information filed with it available to the public at a charge not to exceed actual cost of copying.

Federal Electoral Candidate Information Reports - N.C. Gen. Stat. § 163-278.30

Candidates for nomination in a party primary or for election in a general or special election to the United States House of Representatives, Senate, President, and Vice-President must file with the State Board of Elections all reports required by the Federal Election Campaign Act of 1971. These reports are made available by the Board for public inspection and copying during regular office hours, at the expense of the individual requesting inspection or copying. These reports are to be made available for inspection and copying as soon as practicable, but not later than the end of the day during which they are received.

Records of Receipts and Expenditures from Governmental Election Funds - N.C. Gen. Stat. § 163-278.43(a)

The State chairman of each political party receiving funds from the Political Parties Fund or the Presidential Election Year Candidates Fund are required to keep records of receipts and expenditures of fund monies. This record is to be centrally located and available for public inspection at reasonable hours.

Voter Registration for Municipal Annexations and Incorporations - N.C. Gen. Stat. § 163-288.2(a)

For referenda and elections related to the incorporation of new municipalities or the annexation of territory to existing municipalities, the county board of elections determines which voters are eligible to vote. The board may do so by one of two methods. With one of these methods, the board prepares a list of registered voters living within the affected area. This list is made available for public inspection before the vote, and registered voters in the affected area who are not on the list may add their names to the list.

Division of Veteran Affairs - N.C. Gen. Stat. §§ 165-11 and 165-11.1

The Division of Veteran Affairs in the Department of Administration assists veterans and their beneficiaries in obtaining veterans' benefits. Whenever representatives of the Department request public records from State and local agencies for this purpose, those agencies are to provide those records free of charge.[50] This section does not authorize the disclosure of records designated by law as privileged or confidential. These restricted records may only be disclosed as provided by law.

No records of the Division of Veteran Affairs may be disclosed or used for anything but official purposes. No records of the Division may be disclosed, destroyed or used in violation of federal law or regulation.

Public Policy Exceptions to Public Records Law Disclosure Requirements - *S.E.T.A. UNC-CH, Inc. v. Huffines*, 101 N.C. App. 292, 399 S.E.2d 340 (1991); *News & Observer Pub. Co. v. Poole*, 330 N.C. 465, 412 S.E.2d 7 (1992)

It is generally assumed that government records falling within the definition of public records are subject to public disclosure unless there is a specific exemption for them in the North Carolina General Statutes.

The only appellate case recognizing a public policy exception to the public records law is *S.E.T.A. UNC-CH, Inc. v. Huffines*, 101 N.C. App. 292, 399 S.E.2d 340 (1991). In *Huffines*, an animal rights group sought disclosure of applications for approval to do proposed experimental research on animals at a State university. The university refused to disclose the applications, basing its refusal in part on a public policy argument that disclosure might subject researchers to violence and harassment and thus have a chilling effect on university research.

The requirement that agencies provide veterans' records free of charge still applies to all agencies, including clerks of court offices, even after the 1967 enactment of a statutory schedule of fees that clerks of court ordinarily charge for providing copies of their records. 40 N.C.A.G. 636 (1969)

The North Carolina Court of Appeals refused to recognize a public policy exception for all of the information in the applications. The Court held that information describing the proposed experiments was public records and should be disclosed.

However, the court said it was sensitive to the needs of researchers to protect their privacy and the privacy of their staffs. Without identifying any statutory basis for its decision, the Court concluded that public policy allowed the university to withhold the names, telephone numbers, addresses, department names, and departmental experience of researchers and their staffs.

Also without citing any statutory basis, the Court ruled that research applications that were not approved also did not have to be disclosed. The Court did not explain the public policy interest involved in this exception. Apparently, the court was simply exercising its discretion in determining how much information the animal rights group reasonably needed or deserved.

A year after the *Huffines* decision, the North Carolina Supreme Court took a much stricter approach to nonstatutory public policy exceptions to the disclosure requirements of the public records law. In *News & Observer Pub. Co. v. Poole*, 330 N.C. 465, 412 S.E.2d 7 (1992), the Court rejected several public policy arguments for withholding government documents. Rejecting an argument that State Bureau of Investigation records should be exempt from disclosure even after they have been turned over to another government agency, the Court said, "The legislature knows how to extend the scope of protection of confidential records beyond the confines of the agency which maintains them . . . Where the legislature has not included such broad protection . . . we will not engraft it." *Id.*, at 474.

Ruling that there is no public records exception for minutes of meetings of an agency not subject to the open meetings law, the Court said, "We decline to create such a broad exception to the Public Records Law where the legislature has not elected to do so." *Id.*, at 478.

The Court declined to address whether all communications between government agencies and their attorneys are subject to the traditional common law attorney-client privilege, and are thus not subject to disclosure under the public records law. Instead, the Court relied strictly on the public records law provision, which says only that written communications from attorneys to their government clients are exempt. *Id.*, at 482-483.

Finally, the Court rejected an argument that draft reports by government officials should be exempted from public disclosure based on a public policy "deliberative process privilege." The Court said, "Our statute contains no deliberative process privilege exception. Whether one should be made is a question for the legislature, not the Court." *Id.*, at 484.

To summarize its holdings in *Poole*, the Court stated:

> "In conclusion, we hold that in the absence of clear statutory exemption or exception, documents falling within the definition of "public records" in the Public Records Law must be made available for public inspection." *Id.,* at 486.

Part III
Exemptions from the Public Records Law and the Open Meetings Law for Certain Counties and Municipalities

The public records and open meetings laws apply to local governments within North Carolina. However, the North Carolina General Assembly has permitted some counties, cities and towns to pass ordinances that exempt certain documents and meetings from these laws. Part III of the manual discusses the kinds of records and meetings that local governments have been permitted to exempt, and it lists the counties, cities and towns that have been given these exemptions.

Admissions Fee Tax Returns

The General Assembly has authorized the City of Greensboro to assess a tax on admissions fees for entertainment, amusement or athletic events at city facilities. The city is authorized to exempt from the public records law tax returns filed pursuant to this tax assessment. 1989 N.C. Sess. Laws Ch. 383, § 1

Board of Education Discussions of Voting Rights Litigation

The General Assembly has authorized some counties and municipalities to merge their county and municipal school administrative units. The school boards in some of these jurisdictions have been authorized to hold closed session discussions about litigation or potential litigation involving the Voting Rights Act. Jurisdictions given this authority are:

Edgecombe County - Tarboro	1991 N.C. Sess. Laws Ch. 404, §§ 3, 4 and 5
Franklin County - Franklinton	1993 N.C. Sess. Laws Ch. 341, §§ 4, 5 and 6

Discrimination Investigations and Proceedings

The General Assembly has authorized several counties and municipalities to adopt ordinances prohibiting discrimination. These jurisdictions are authorized to provide in their ordinances that certain discrimination complaint investigation records are exempt from the public records law. Some of these jurisdictions are authorized to exempt discrimination complaint investigation and conciliation proceedings from the open meetings law. These provisions apply in the following jurisdictions:

Durham County	1993 N.C. Sess. Laws ch. 227, §§ 8 and 9

Orange County	1993 N.C. Sess. Laws ch. 358, § 14
New Hanover County	1981 N.C. Sess. Laws ch. 960, §§ 7 and 8
Durham (city)	1993 N.C. Sess. Laws ch. 227, §§ 8 and 9
Fayetteville	1989 N.C. Sess. Laws ch. 355, § 1
Gastonia	1985 N.C. Sess. Laws ch. 902, §§ 7 and 8
Greensboro	1987 N.C. Sess. Laws ch. 51, § 1

Food and Beverage Tax Returns

The General Assembly has authorized some North Carolina counties and municipalities to assess food and beverage taxes. The following jurisdictions have been authorized to exempt from the public records law tax returns filed pursuant to this tax levy:

Cumberland County	1993 N.C. Sess. Laws ch. 413, § 5
Hillsborough	1993 N.C. Sess. Laws ch. 449, § 1

Official City Map Open for Inspection

The General Assembly passed a law saying that the official map of the City of Gastonia is kept permanently in the office of the City Clerk and is available for public inspection.   1991 N.C. Sess. Laws ch. 557, §

Room Occupancy and Tourism Development Tax Returns

The General Assembly has authorized many North Carolina counties and municipalities to assess room occupancy taxes or tourism development taxes for rooms in hotels, motels, inns, and other overnight accommodations. The following jurisdictions are authorized to exempt from the public records law tax returns filed pursuant these tax levies:

Counties

Alamance County	1987 N.C. Sess. Laws ch. 950, § 1
Alleghany County	1991 N.C. Sess. Laws ch. 162, § 1
Ashe County	1991 N.C. Sess. Laws ch. 163, § 1
Avery County	1993 N.C. Sess. Laws ch. 472, § 1
Burke County	1989 N.C. Sess. Laws ch. 422, § 1
Cabarrus County	1989 N.C. Sess. Laws ch. 658, § 1
Carteret County	1989 N.C. Sess. Laws ch. 171, § 8

Chatham County	1993 N.C. Sess. Laws ch. 642, § 1
Chowan County	1989 N.C. Sess. Laws ch. 174, § 1
Cleveland County	1989 N.C. Sess. Laws ch. 173, § 1
Currituck County	1987 N.C. Sess. Laws ch. 209, § 1
Dare County	1991 N.C. Sess. Laws ch. 177, § 1
Davidson County	1993 N.C. Sess. Laws ch. 453, § 1
Davie County	1989 N.C. Sess. Laws ch. 928, § 1
Duplin County	1987 N.C. Sess. Laws ch. 317, § 1
Gaston County	1987 N.C. Sess. Laws ch. 618, § 1
Granville County	1987 N.C. Sess. Laws ch. 377, § 1
Henderson County	1987 N.C. Sess. Laws ch. 172, § 5
Hertford County	1987 N.C. Sess. Laws ch. 979, § 1
Lee County	1987 N.C. Sess. Laws ch. 538, § 1
Lenoir County	1987 N.C. Sess. Laws ch. 561, § 1
Lincoln County	1993 N.C. Sess. Laws ch. 549, § 1
Martin County	1991 N.C. Sess. Laws ch. 80, § 1
Mitchell County	1987 N.C. Sess. Laws ch. 141, § 1
Nash County	1987 N.C. Sess. Laws ch. 32, § 1
Pasquotank County	1987 N.C. Sess. Laws ch. 175, § 1
Pender County	1987 N.C. Sess. Laws ch. 175, § 1
Pitt County	1991 N.C. Sess. Laws ch. 577, § 5
Rowan County	1987 N.C. Sess. Laws ch. 379, § 1
Rutherford County	1987 N.C. Sess. Laws ch. 577, § 5

Vance County	1987 N.C. Sess. Laws ch. 1067, § 1
Wake County	1987 N.C. Sess. Laws ch. 594. § 9
Washington County	1991 N.C. Sess. Laws ch. 821, § 1
Yancey County	1987 N.C. Sess. Laws ch. 140, § 1

Municipalities and Townships

Albemarle	1991 N.C. Sess. Laws ch. 915, § 1
Averasboro	1987 N.C. Sess. Laws ch. 142, § 1
Bald Head Island	1991 N.C. Sess. Laws ch. 664, § 2
Banner Elk	1989 N.C. Sess. Laws ch. 318, § 2
Beech Mountain	1987 N.C. Sess. Laws ch. 376, § 2
Blowing Rock	1987 N.C. Sess. Laws ch. 171, § 1
Boone	1987 N.C. Sess. Laws ch. 170, § 1
Cary	1989 N.C. Sess. Laws ch. 874, § 1
Caswell Beach	1991 N.C. Sess. Laws ch. 664, § 1
Columbus	1991 N.C. Sess. Laws ch. 632, § 1
Conover	1987 N.C. Sess. Laws ch. 319, § 1
Elizabeth City	1987 N.C. Sess. Laws ch. 175, § 1
Garner	1989 N.C. Sess. Laws ch. 660, § 1
Hickory	1987 N.C. Sess. Laws ch. 319, § 1
Holden Beach	1987 N.C. Sess. Laws ch. 963, § 1
Kinston	1993 N.C. Sess. Laws ch. 648, §1
Lexington	1993 N.C. Sess. Laws ch. 602, § 1
Mooresville	1991 N.C. Sess. Laws ch. 296, § 1
Oriental	1993 N.C. Sess. Laws ch. 695, § 1

Southport	1989 N.C. Sess. Laws ch. 639, § 1
Sunset Beach	1987 N.C. Sess. Laws ch. 956, § 1
Wake Forest	1989 N.C. Sess. Laws ch. 604, § 1
Washington	1991 N.C. Sess. Laws ch. 158, § 1
Yaupon Beach	1991 N.C. Sess. Laws ch. 820, § 1

Part IV
Table of Cases

Advance Publications, Inc. v. Elizabeth City, 53 N.C. App. 504, 281 S.E.2d 69 (1981)

- A letter from a city's contractor to the city manager was a public record.
- Corporations are "persons" who may inspect public records.

Carnahan v. Reed 53 N.C. App. 589, 281 S.E.2d 408 (1981)

- The widow of a prisoner who committed suicide was not permitted to see Department of Correction psychiatric evaluations of her former husband.

Cohn v. Wilkes General Hosp., 127 F.R.D. 117 (W.D.N.C. 1989)

- A public hospital board's closed session discussions on medical staff privileges were not subject to discovery.

Coulter v. (City of Newton)(Newton), 100 N.C. App. 523, 397 S.E.2d 244 (1990)

- A suit challenging an allegedly improper action taken by a city board during a closed session was barred because the plaintiffs filed suit more than 45 days after the board's action was disclosed.

Dockside Discotheque (, Inc.) v. Board of Adjustment (of the Town of Southern Pines), 115 N.C. App. 303, 444 S.E.2d 451 (1994)

- A board of adjustment's closed session discussion of a disco owner's request for permission to have topless entertainment at his disco did not have a significant impact on the board's later decision to deny permission, and the Court refused to declare the board's action null and void.

Durham Herald Co., Inc. v. County of Durham, 334 N.C. 677, 435 S.E.2d 317 (1993)

- Applications from people seeking to replace the sheriff were confidential personnel information.

Durham Herald Co. v. North Carolina Low-Level Radioactive Waste Management Authority, 110 N.C. App. 607, 430 S.E.2d 441 (1993)

- Documents produced by private companies for a waste management authority were not yet public records since they had not yet been received by the authority.

Eggimann v. Wake County Board of Education, 22 N.C. App. 459, 206 S.E.2d 754 (1974)

- A school board's private discussions of school site selection were not void since the board later voted on the issue at an open meeting.

Elkin Tribune v. Yadkin County Board of Commissioners, (but see *State v. McKoy,* 331 N.C. 731) 331 N.C. 734, 417 S.E.2d 465 (1992)

- Applications for a county manager position were confidential personnel information.

Goble v. Bounds, 281 N.C. 307, 188 S.E.2d 347 (1972)

- Department of Correction and Parole Commission records relating to possible parole of prisoners are confidential.

Housing Authority of Raleigh v. Montgomery, 55 N.C. App. 422, 286 S.E.2d 114 (1982)

- A housing authority refused to disclose appraisals to a landowner whose land was the subject of a condemnation proceeding. The Court held that the alleged public records law violation could not be raised as an affirmative defense by the landowner in the condemnation proceeding.

In re Hayes, 111 N.C. App. 384, 432 S.E.2d 862 (1993)

- Requiring open commitment hearings for insanity acquitees, while requiring the closing of other commitment hearings, did not violate the defendant's constitutional rights.

In re Southern Bell Tel. & Tel. Co., 30 N.C. App. 585, 227 S.E.2d 645 (1976)

- The Attorney General got statements from corporate employees during an investigation into alleged misuse of funds by the corporation. Based on the employees' privacy interests, the lower court properly issued a protective order requiring the Attorney General not to disclose the employees' statements prior to prosecution.

In re Norwell, 293 N.C. 235, 237 S.E.2d 246 (1977)

- A judge was censured for disposing of cases out of court.

In re Peoples, 296 N.C. 109, 250 S.E.2d 890 (1978)

- A judge was censured for disposing of cases out of court.

In re Sullivan, 112 N.C. App. 795, 436 S.E.2d 862 (1993)

- The Board of Medical Examiners has some responsibility to ensure its records on licensees are accurate, and a doctor had the right to petition the board to expunge false and prejudicial information in his records.

Jacksonville Daily News Co. v. Onslow County Bd. of Educ., 113 N.C. App. 127, 439 S.E.2d 607 (1993)

- A school board violated the open meetings law by discussing and approving retroactive pay raises for its members in private discussions.

Leak v. High Point City Council, 25 N.C. App. 394, 213 S.E.2d 386 (1975)

- There was no justification for excluding live radio and TV coverage of city council investigative hearings on police corruption.

Lewis v. White, 287 S.E.2d 134, 287 N.C. 625 (1975)

- The wording for a request for injunctive relief in an open meetings lawsuit was too broad.

Moore v. Beaufort County, 936 F.2d 159 (4th Cir. 1991)

- A county board's closed session instructions to its attorney to settle a lawsuit gave the attorney binding authority to settle the suit, and the resulting settlement was valid.

North Carolina Elec. Membership Corp. v. North Carolina Dep't of Economic & Community Dev., 108 N.C. App. 711, 425 S.E.2d 440 (1993)

- A company's financial forecast documents and feasibility studies submitted to a State agency in connection with a federal grant application were confidential trade secrets.

News & Observer Pub. Co. v. Poole, 330 N.C. 465, 412 S.E.2d 7 (1992)

- A preliminary draft of a government commission report was not exempt from public records law disclosure requirements.

- Government agencies not subject to the open meetings law may not claim that law's exemption from disclosure of minutes of closed sessions.

- The public records and open meetings laws are discrete statutes. Exemption from the open meetings law does not necessarily imply exemption from the public records law.

- State employee personnel information is confidential only when it is first gathered by the employee's own agency.

- With regard to attorney-client communications, the public records law only exempts from disclosure written communication from attorneys to their government clients.

- In the absence of a clear statutory exemption, documents falling within the definition of "public records" must be made available for public inspection.

News & Observer Pub. Co. v. Wake County Hospital System, Inc., 55 N.C. App. 1, 284 S.E.2d 542 (1981), *cert. denied*, 305 N.C. 302, 291 S.E.2d 151 (1982)

- A nonprofit hospital corporation was subject to the public records law since its county retained control over the hospital's board, property and finances.

- Public records include documents government agencies make or collect at their discretion in carrying on public business, not just records that are required by law to be made or collected.

North Carolina Press Asso. v. Spangler, 87 N.C. App. 169, 360 S.E.2d 138 (1987)

- The fact that a public university's documents were preliminary, intergovernmental communications did not justify a refusal to disclose them under the public records law.

- Government agencies may not withhold public records from disclosure based on the agency's belief that immediate release would not be prudent or timely.

- The awarding of attorney's fees against a government agency in a public records lawsuit depends on whether the agency had substantial justification in denying access. The agency has the burden of proving that it had substantial justification. In this case, the agency lacked substantial justification in denying disclosure of records based on its belief that preliminary working papers and intergovernmental communications should be exempt from the public records law for public policy reasons.

Northampton County Drainage Dist. Number One v. Bailey, 92 N.C. App. 68, 373 S.E.2d 560 (1988)

- A drainage district was a political subdivision of the State with quasi-judicial and administrative authority and was a public body subject to the open meetings law.

- Landowners did not make a timely challenge under the open meetings law to fees assessed by the drainage district at an improper meeting, and they could not make a later due process challenge to the assessments.

Paine v. Baker, 595 F.2d 197 (4th Cir. N.C. 1979),cert. denied, 444 U.S. 925, 100 S. Ct. 263, 62 L.Ed.2d 181 (1979)

- There is no general right of access to prison records. However, a prisoner has a limited right of access to his prison records if a false item is relied upon in a way that violates his constitutional rights.

Piedmont Publishing Co. v. City of Winston-Salem, 334 N.C. 595, 434 S.E.2d 176 (1993)

- Criminal defendants and the public cannot use the public records law to get information that defendants are not entitled to get criminal discovery.

S.E.T.A. UNC-CH, Inc. v. Huffines, 101 N.C. App. 292, 399 S.E.2d 340 (1991)

- A public university could not refuse to disclose experimental animal research applications on the public policy ground that disclosure might subject researchers to harassment and have a chilling effect on university research.

- Personal information about researchers could be withheld from disclosure based on the researchers' privacy interests.

- Disapproved applications could be withheld from disclosure.

- Nonpublic information in otherwise public records may be redacted before disclosure.

- The awarding of attorney's fees against a government agency in a public records lawsuit depends on whether the agency had substantial justification for withholding the records. The test for substantial justification is not whether the court ultimately finds the agency's reasons for nondisclosure were correct. The test is whether a reasonable person could think the agency was correct, given the existing law and facts. In this case, an attorney's fees award was rejected because the agency had substantial justification to believe release of the documents might be exempt because their release could have a chilling effect on university research and academic freedom.

Sheppard v. Sheppard, 38 N.C. App. 712, 248 S.E.2d 871 (1978)

- Records of an adoption case obtained from the parents' former attorney were inadmissible in a later child custody case because the records had not been obtained in a special statutory proceeding designed to ensure adoption records are released only in appropriate circumstances.

State v. Shaw, 305 N.C. 327, 289 S.E.2d 325 (1982)

- The physician-patient privilege does not apply to communications between optometrists and their patients.

Weston v. Carolina Medicorp, 102 N.C. App. 370, 402 S.E.2d 653 (1991)

- A hospital may require doctors admitting patients who are HIV positive to place those patients on blood and body fluid isolation, even though this identifies those patients as potentially HIV infectious.

Whisenhunt v. Zammit, 86 N.C. App. 425, 358 S.E.2d 114 (1987)

- A medical malpractice plaintiff could not require the production of a county hospital's credentialing file on a doctor.

Winfas Inc. v. Region P Human Dev. Agency, 64 N.C. App. 724, 308 S.E.2d 99 (1983)

- The fact that a human development agency created by a county later became a nonprofit corporation did not alter its status as a public body for the purposes of the open meetings law.

Wright v. County of Macon, 64 N.C. App. 718, 308 S.E.2d 97 (1983)

- A county board of commissioners complied with meeting notice requirements by adjourning a regular meeting on August 2 and posting notice on August 13 that the meeting would be reconvened on August 16.

WSOC Television, Inc. v. State ex rel. Attorney General, (*In re Belk*)107 N.C. App. 448, 420 S.E.2d 682 (1992)

- Confidential involuntary commitment hearings are constitutional. Neither a television station nor the public have a constitutional right to have access to an involuntary commitment hearing or the records of the person who was the subject of the hearing.

Part V
North Carolina Attorney General Opinions

29 N.C.A.G. 697 (1948)

- Petitions for county alcoholic beverage elections are pub ic records.

31 N.C.A.G. 82 (1951)

- The records of proceedings and the register of all examination applicants of the State Board of Examiners of Plumbing, Heating and Fire Sprinkler Contractors are public records subject to inspection.

34 N.C.A.G. 132 (1958)

- Clinical records of individual patients treated in public health departments are not public records and are not subject to public inspection.

34 N.C.A.G. 132 (1958)

- Documents, papers, and letters other than clinical records accumulated by local health officers and health department are public records.

37 N.C.A.G. 85 (1962

- County and municipal property tax listing abstracts are public records subject to public examination.

40 N.C.A.G. 636 (1969)

- People who want information from the government are permitted to examine existing records. The public records law does not require government agencies to extract information from its existing records and rewrite it or compile it in another form for public inspection.

40 N.C.A.G. 636 (1969)

- Clerks of court may not charge fees to provide public records to the Division of Veteran Affairs when the records are requested by the Division to assist veterans and their beneficiaries in obtaining veterans' benefits.

40 N.C.A.G. 709 (1969)

- Access to public records should be permitted regardless of the announced or unannounced purposes for which the information acquired from the records will be used.
- County auditors' registers of people receiving public assistance are public records.

40 N.C.A.G. 713 (1969)

- It is permissible for Departments of Social Services to supply information on children receiving AFDC benefits to a nonprofit group commissioned to do a survey of children's services.

41 N.C.A.G. 199 (1971)

- Public records include not only documents specifically required by law to be made or received by a government agency, but also any documents made by government officials in their public employment capacity.
- Textbook lists submitted by departments of a state university to the university bookstore are public records, and these lists may be inspected by private textbook vendors.

41 N.C.A.G. 407 (1971)

- Police department arrest and disposition records are public records.

41 N.C.A.G. 666 (1971)

- A facility for people with mental disabilities must disclose confidential client information if ordered to do so by a clerk of court.

42 N.C.A.G. 229 (1973)

- Any person may demand inspection of public records even if his motives are based on mere speculation or idle curiosity.
- A person inspecting public records may make copies with his own clerical assistants.
- Investigation papers compiled by school counselors are privileged records.
- Public school teacher contracts are public records.

- Tax returns of public school teachers are confidential and may not be disclosed by school boards.

43 N.C.A.G. 274 (1973)

- Municipal books and papers, such as budgets, bank statements, tax levies, utility accounts and minutes of meetings are all public records subject to inspection.

44 N.C.A.G. 305 (1975)

- Juvenile arrest records are confidential.

45 N.C.A.G. 55 (1975)

- Tax appraisal cards being worked on for a county by a private contractor were not public records because they had not yet been turned over to the county.

45 N.C.A.G. 188 (1975)

- Applications for licensure and other documentary licensing information received by the Board of Examiners for Speech and Language Pathologists and Audiologists are public records subject to inspection.

46 N.C.A.G. 20 (1976)

- The State Personnel Commission may not use a closed session to deliberate upon and approve a county's plan to deviate from the Commission's standard salary ranges.

46 N.C.A.G. 142 (1976)

- Special counsel representing a patient at a facility for people with mental disabilities is entitled to inspect and receive copies of the patient's records.

47 N.C.A.G. 141 (1977)

- A State agency may not inform the news media that an employee is under investigation, the reasons for the investigation or the results of the investigation. If the employee is suspended, the agency may only tell the media the date of the employee's most recent suspension, but not the reasons for the suspension.

47 N.C.A.G. 164 (1978)

- Information disclosed at a State employee's departmental grievance hearing may not be disclosed to the media. Information disclosed at the employee's appeal hearing before the State Personnel Commission may be disclosed to the media since the hearing is public. The nature of discipline taken against a State employee may not be made public.

48 N.C.A.G. 32 (1978)

- Licensed chiropractors have access to their patients' X-ray and laboratory records at public supported hospitals.

48 N.C.A.G. 84 (1979)

- State agencies are required to provide to members of the General Assembly, upon request, all information in their records or that is ascertainable from their records, including personnel information. A member of the General Assembly requesting the information need not be a member of an investigatory committee looking into an issue in order to access the information.

48 N.C.A.G. 85 (1979)

- State, county and municipal personnel directors must release confidential information about their employees to the Department of Human Resources to aid it in child support enforcement efforts.

49 N.C.A.G. 17 (1979)

- Statutes calling for the expunction of juvenile records apply to juvenile adjudications in which several misdemeanor charges were consolidated for trial and judgment.

49 N.C.A.G. 61 (1979)

- Departments of Social Services may release records of Title XX public assistance recipients to the Evaluation Section of the Department of Human Resources in order for that section to conduct a study requested by the General Assembly.

49 N.C.A.G. 198 (1980)

- Departments of Social Services may not release protective service case records of juveniles to a volunteer advisory group appointed by a chief judge to advise the juvenile court on custody of children in foster homes.

51 N.C.A.G. 17 (1981)

- Patients at facilities for people with mental disabilities must be notified they have the right to object to disclosure of their records to the Department of Human Resources. It is insufficient for the Department to post notices to this effect.

Patients should be given individual printed notices upon admission.

52 N.C.A.G. 85 (1983)

- Home addresses of State employees may be obtained from State personnel offices by ad valorem tax collectors, since they only collect taxes due and do not conduct investigations into the employees' tax liability.

53 N.C.A.G. 108 (1980)

- Law enforcement officers may have access to public assistance records at Departments of Social Services offices, without subpoenas, search warrants or court orders, to investigate allegations of criminal fraud by recipients in obtaining assistance.

54 N.C.A.G. 84 (1985)

- A local board of education need not state in a public record or in a public meeting the reasons why it decided not to renew a teacher's contract. The reasons may be indicated in a teacher's personnel file, which is confidential.

57 N.C.A.G. 38 (1987)

- The North Carolina Medical Database Commission's use of patient social security numbers to ensure the accuracy of its information is permitted by federal law.

58 N.C.A.G. 33 (1988)

- Law enforcement officers must forward collision investigation reports involving juveniles to the Division of Motor Vehicles. Collision reports, in and of themselves, do not contain allegations of criminal offenses by juveniles.

59 N.C.A.G. 4 (1989)

- The Financial Privacy Act applies to customers who open accounts at financial institutions using fictitious names, even if a financial institution is the victim of an alleged crime by the customer.

60 N.C.A.G. 76 (1991)

- Except as required by law or rule, individual test scores, and applications and related materials (including references) received by the North Carolina Board of for the Licensing of Geologists are confidential.

Part VI
Some Common Public Records and Where They Can Be Found

	Statutory Reference
Agriculture, Department of	
Livestock Brands	§ 80-59
Clerks of Superior Court	
Adoption Orders	N.C. Gen. Stat. § 48-24
Assumed Business Names	§ 66-68 and § 66-69
Civil Actions	§ 7A-109
Court Minutes	§ 7A-109
Criminal Actions	§ 7A-109
Drainage Assessments	§ 156-103
Election Results	§ 163-176
Executors and Administrators of Estates, Appointment	§ 28A-6
Guardians	§ 35A-1206 and § 35A-1231(a)
Judgments	§ 7A-109
Juvenile Actions	§ 7A-109
Legitimization of Children, Orders for	§ 49-10
Liens	§ 7A-109
Lis Pendens	§ 7A-109
Name Changes	§ 101-7
Renunciation of Property Succession Rights	§ 31B-2(c)
Search Warrants	§ 15A-257
Wills	§ 31-20

Elections, County Boards of
    Absentee Ballot Registers .... § 163-228 and § 163-248
    Election Precinct Maps .... § 163-128(b)
    Election Results .... § 163-177
    Voter Registration Records .... § 163-66
Inspections Departments
    Underground Utilities .... § 87-111
Motor Vehicles, Division of
    Drivers License Records .... § 20-26
    Motor Vehicle Collision Reports... § 20-166.1(i)
    Motor Vehicle Registration .... § 20-56
Register of Deeds Offices
    Annexation (Municipal), Maps and Ordinances .... §§ 160A-29, 160A-39, 160A-51
    Assumed Business Names... § 161-14.01
    Bankruptcy Records .... § 47-29
    Birth Certificates .... § 130A-99
    Conditional Sales Contracts .... § 47-47-20
    Condominium Declarations... § 47C-2-101
    Conservation Agreements .... § 121-41
    Corporate Merger or Consolidation Certificates.................................... § 47-18.1
    Crop Sales Contracts .... § 25-2-107
    Decrees of title to land... § 43-13
    Death Certificates .... § 130A-99
    Deeds of Trust .... §§ 45 and 47-20
    Easement Deeds .... § 47-27
    Electric Membership Corporations, Mergers and Consolidations .... § 117-43
    Eminent Domain - Memorandum of Action by Landowner .... § 40A-51
    Foreclosures... § 45
    Gift Deeds.. § 47-26
    Grantor and Grantee Indexes .... § 47-18

Hazardous Substance and Waste Disposal, Permits and Sites	§§ 130A-301 and 130A-310.8
Incorporations	§ 161-14.01
Land Conveyances	§ 47-18
Land Conveyance Contracts	§ 47-18
Leases of Real Estate	§ 47-18
Marriage Certificates	§ 130A-110
Marriage Licenses	§ 51-18
Marriage Settlements	§ 47-25
Military Discharges	§ 47-2
Mineral Sales Contracts	§ 25-2-107
Mortgages	§ 45
Options to Purchase Land	§ 47-18
Partitions of Land	§ 46-20
Partnership Certificates	§ 161-14.01
Petroleum Leases	§ 113-414
Plats	§ 47-30
Powers of Attorney	§ 47-28
Renunciation of Real Property Rights	§ 31B-2(d)
Subdivisions	§ 47-30
Timber Sales Contracts	§ 25-2-107
Time Shares	§ 47C-1-109
Title Transfers (land titles)	§ 43-13
Transportation Department Land Condemnation, Memoranda Of Action	§§ 136-104 and 136-111
Underground Utilities	§§ 87-109 and 87-110
Unit Ownership	§ 47-13
Wetlands - Orders of Secretary of DEHNR Restricting Development Activity in Coastal Wetlands	§ 113-230(c)

Secretary of State

> Annexation (Municipal), Maps and Ordinances.......................... §§ 160A-29, 160A-39, 160A-51, 160A-58.7
>
> Appointments to State Boards, Commissions, etc............................ § 147-36(14)
>
> Business Corporations: Articles of Incorporation, Annual Reports, and Other Corporate Documents.. § 55
>
> Business Licenses - Information, Requirements and Forms .... § 147-54.13
>
> Election Results... §§ 163-192(c) and 163-195
>
> Electric Membership Corporations, Mergers and Consolidations .... § 117-43
>
> Land Grants from the State of North Carolina, Plats, Surveys and Abstracts... §§ 8-6 through 8-9
>
> Land Grant Judgments .... § 146-62
>
> Limited Liability Companies: Articles of Organization, Annual Reports, and Other Company Documents .... § 57C
>
> Limited Partnerships... § 59-201
>
> Nonprofit Corporations: Articles of Incorporation, Annual Reports, and other Corporate Documents... § 55A
>
> Oaths of Public Officials .... § 147-36(13)
>
> Occupational Licensing Board Annual Reports .... § 93B-2
>
> Oyster Grants .... § 147-41
>
> Professional Corporations: Articles of Incorporation, Annual Reports, and Other Corporate Documents... § 55B-3
>
> Real Property Conveyances to the State... § 147-39
>
> Reports of State Officers .... § 147-43
>
> Traffic, Parking and Motor Vehicle Ordinances of the University of North Carolina.. § 116-44.4(l)
>
> Wills.. § 8-29

Vital Statistics, State Registrar of

> Birth Certificates .... § 130A-93
>
> Death Certificates .... § 130A-93

Part VII
State Government Offices

Principal State Departments

ADMINISTRATION, DEPARTMENT OF

    Mailing address: 1304 Mail Service Center, Raleigh, North Carolina 27699-1304
    Street address: 217 West Jones Street, Raleigh

Public Information

    ADA (Americans with Disabilities Act) - Information and assistance to businesses only
    Bid Information
    Child Advocacy - Councils and Commissions
    Disabilities - Protection and advocacy services
    Energy - Energy programs and services
    Financial Aid Directory - College scholarship and loan information for American Indians
    Housing - Fair Housing to prevent discrimination
    Historically Underutilized Businesses Office
    Home Schooling
    Indians - Information about N.C. Indians
    Minority Business Information (HUB Office)
    Private Schools - Information from the office overseeing private schools
    Procurement Opportunities
    Real Property - Purchasing, leasing and selling of real property by the state
    Veterans - Benefits and information for military veterans and their dependents
    Women Business Opportunities - (HUB Office)
    Women's Issues - General Information
    Youth Programs - General information

YLA - Youth Legislative Assembly
Youth Mini Grants - General information
Domestic Violence Commission
Veterans Affairs Commission

ADMINISTRATIVE HEARINGS, OFFICE OF

Mailing address: 6714 Mail Service Center, Raleigh, NC 27699-6714
Street address: 424 N Blount St, Raleigh

AGRICULTURE & CONSUMER SERVICES, DEPARTMENT OF

Address: 2 West Edenton Street, Raleigh, NC 27601

Public Information:

Agricultural Statistics
Agronomics
Golden LEAF Foundation
Market News
Plant Industry
Veterinary

ARCHIVES, STATE

Fax: (919) 733-1354

Address: Public Services Branch, 4614 Mail Service Center, Raleigh, NC 27699-4614

ATTORNEY GENERAL, OFFICE OF THE

Mailing address: North Carolina Department of Justice, P.O. Box 629, Raleigh, NC 27602-0629

Consumer Protection Section: (919) 716-6000 (voice), 716-6050 (fax), 716-6001 (auto)
Criminal Justice Standards: (919) 716-6470 (voice), 716-6752 (fax)

DCI/Audit Training Section: (919) 662-4509 (voice), 919-662-4619 (fax)

Environmental Protection Division: (919) 716-6600 (voice), 716-6767 (fax)
Labor Section: (919) 716-6680 (voice), 716-6709 (fax)
Law Enforcement Section: (919) 716-6500 (voice), 716-6760 (fax)
Medicaid Investigations Section: (919) 881-2320 (voice), 571-4837 (fax)
NC Justice Academy: (910) 525-4151 (voice), 910-525-5439 (fax)
Private Protective Services / Alarm Licensing Board: (919) 875-3611 (voice), 875-3609 (fax)
Sheriffs' Standards Section: (919) 716-6460 (voice), 716-6753 (fax)
State Bureau of Investigation: (919) 662-4500 (voice), 662-4523 (fax)
Tort Claims Section: (919) 716-6820 (voice), 716-6759 (fax)

COMMERCE, DEPARTMENT OF

Address: 301 North Wilmington Street, Raleigh, NC 27699-4301

The Department of Commerce is the State of North Carolina's lead agency for economic, community and workforce development. The Department also has under its auspices the information technology function for state government and agencies, which regulate commerce in the state.

COURTS, ADMINISTRATIVE OFFICE OF THE

(919) 733-7107

Mailing address: P.O. Box 2448, Raleigh, NC 27602

CRIME CONTROL AND PUBLIC SAFETY, OFFICE OF

Mailing address: 4701 Mail Service Center, Raleigh, N.C. 27699-0601
Street address: 512 N. Salisbury Street, Raleigh

ELECTIONS, STATE BOARD OF

Main Number: (919) 733-7173;
Fax:
    Administration - (919) 715-0135;
    Campaign Reporting - (919) 715-8047;
    Information Systems - (919) 715-1344

Mailing address: P.O. Box 27255, Raleigh, NC 27611-7255
Street address: 506 North Harrington Street, Raleigh, NC 27603

HEALTH AND HUMAN SERVICES, DEPARTMENT OF

Aging, Division of
    Mailing address: 2101 Mail Service Center, Raleigh, NC 27699-2101
    Street address: 693 Palmer Dr., Raleigh

Boards and Commissions, Office of
    Mailing address: 2004 Mail Service Center, Raleigh, NC 27699-2004
    Street address: Adams Building, 101 Blair Drive, Raleigh

Child Development, Division of
    Mailing address: 2201 Mail Service Center, Raleigh, NC 27699-2201
    Street address: 319 Chapanoke Road, Ste 120, Raleigh

Citizen Services, Office of
    Mailing address: 2012 Mail Service Center, Raleigh, NC 27699-2012
    Street address: 1020 Richardson Dr., Raleigh

Health Statistics, State Center for
    Mailing address: 1908 Mail Service Center, Raleigh, NC 27699-1908
    Street address: Cotton Building, 222 N. Dawson, Raleigh

Mental Health, Developmental Disabilities and Substance Abuse Services, Division of
    Mailing address: 3001 Mail Service Center, Raleigh, NC 27699-3001
    Street address: Albemarle Building, 325 N. Salisbury St., Raleigh

Public Affairs, Office of
    Mailing address: 2006 Mail Service Center, Raleigh, NC 27699-2006
    Street address: Adams Building, Dix Campus, 101 Blair Drive, Raleigh

Public Health, Division of
    Mailing address: 1916 Mail Service Center, Raleigh, NC 27699-1916
    Street address: 1330 St. Mary's Street, Raleigh

Social Services, Division of
    Mailing address: 2401 Mail Service Center, Raleigh, NC 27699-2401
    Street address: Albemarle Building, 325 N. Salisbury St., Raleigh

Vital Records
    Mailing address: 1903 Mail Service Center, Raleigh, NC 27699-1903
    Street address: Cooper Bldg., Raleigh

INSURANCE, DEPARTMENT OF

    Mailing address: PO Box 26387, Raleigh, NC 27611

LABOR, DEPARTMENT OF

    (919) 807-2796; 800-NC-LABOR (800-625-2267 In-State N.C. calls only)

    Apprenticeship & Training Bureau: (919) 733-7533
    Research & Policy Development: 919-733-0337, (919) 733-2758
    Consumer Price Index, Injury, Illness and Fatality Statistics Employment Discrimination Bureau (EDB): (919) 807-2823
    Individual Development Accounts (IDAs): (919) 733-1387
    Social program to help people escape from poverty
    Wage and Hour Bureau: (919) 807-2796
        Minimum wage, overtime pay, wage payment (promised wages), youth employment (child labor work permits), medical payment law, Private Personnel and Job Listing Services law, Controlled Substance Examination Regulation Act
    Emergency and General Information: 1-800-NC-LABOR (625-2267 In-State Only); ((919) 807-2796 in the Raleigh area)
    Workplace Accidents or Illnesses: (919) 807-2796
    Mining Industry Accidents or Injuries: (919) 807-2790
    Workplace Fatalities: (919) 807-2796
    Workplace Hazards or Complaints: (919) 807-2796

SECRETARY OF STATE

    Mailing address: North Carolina Department of the Secretary of State, ATTN: (Office/Section), P.O. Box 29622, Raleigh, North Carolina 27626-0622
    Street address: 2 South Salisbury Street, Raleigh, NC 27601-2903

    Notary Public Section: (919) 807-2131
    Trademarks Section: (919) 807-2162; (919) 807-2215 (fax)

STATE AUDITOR, OFFICE OF

(919) 807-7500 voice; (919) 807-7647 fax

Mailing address:	N.C. Office Of The State Auditor, 20601 Mail Service Center, Raleigh, N. C. 27699-0601
Street address:	2 South Salisbury Street, Raleigh

N.C. Office of the State Auditor provides independent evaluations of the State's fiscal accountability and public program performance.

TRANSPORTATION, DEPARTMENT OF

Mailing address:	1503 Mail Service Center, Raleigh, NC 27699-1503
Street address:	1 South Wilmington Street, Raleigh, NC 27611

> Driver's license, vehicle registration or other DMV issues, contact the Division of Motor Vehicles at (919) 715-7000.
>
> DOT issues, or to order publications, contact the DOT Customer Service Office at 1-877-DOT-4YOU (1-877-368-4968) or (919) 733-3109.
>
> Media inquiries, contact the Public Information Office at (919) 733-2522.

UNIVERSITY OF NORTH CAROLINA (SYSTEM)

(919) 962-1000

Mailing address:	P.O. Box 2688, Chapel Hill, North Carolina 27515
Street address:	910 Raleigh Road, Chapel Hill, North Carolina 27515

State Licensing Agencies

Board of CPA Examiners
(919) 733-4222; fax 4209
PO Box 12827, Raleigh, NC
27605-2827

Acupuncture Licensing Board
(919) 773-0530
893 US Hwy. 70 West, Ste. 202,
Garner, NC 27529

Alarm Systems Licensing Board
(919) 875-3611
1631 Midtown Place, Ste. 104,
Raleigh, NC 27609

Appraisal Board
(919) 420-7920
PO Box 20500, Raleigh, NC 27619

Board of Architecture
(919) 733-9544
127 W Hargett St., Suite 304, Raleigh,
NC 27601

Board of Athletic Trainer Examiners
(919) 821-4980
PO Box 10769, Raleigh, NC 27605

Auctioneer Licensing Board
(919) 981-5066
1001 Navaho Drive, Suite 105,
Raleigh, NC 27609

Commissioner of Banks
(919) 733-3016
4309 Mail Service Ctr, Raleigh, NC
27699-4309

Board of Barber Examiners
(919) 715-1159
2321 Crabtree Blvd., Ste. 110,
Raleigh, NC 27604

Board of Chiropractic Examiners
704-793-1342
174 Church Street, Concord, NC
28025

Board of Cosmetic Arts
(919) 733-4117
1201 Front St., Suite 110, Raleigh,
NC 27609

Board of Licensed Professional
Counselors
(919) 661-0820
PO Box 21005, Raleigh, NC 27619

Board of Dental Examiners
(919) 678-8223
15100 Weston Pkwy, Ste. 101, Cary,
NC 27513

Board of Dietetics/Nutrition
(919) 779-7154; 800-849-2936
P.O. Box 1509, Garner, NC 27529

Board of Examiners of Electrical
Contractors: (919) 733-9042
PO Box 18727, Raleigh, NC 27619

Board of Electrolysis Examiners
336-574-1414
300 East Wendover Avenue,
Greensboro, NC 27415-3626

Board of Examiners for Engineers and
Surveyors
(919) 841-4000
310 West Millbrook Rd, Raleigh,
NC 27609

Board of Registration for Foresters
(919) 772-5883
PO Box 27393, Raleigh, NC 27611

Board for General Contractors
(919) 571-4183
PO Box 17187, Raleigh, NC 27619

Board for Licensed Geologists
(919) 850-9669; fax (919) 872-1598
PO Box 41225, Raleigh, NC 27629-1225

Board of Hearing Aid Dealers and Fitters
(919) 981-5105
3733 Benson Drive, Raleigh, NC 27609

Home Inspectors Licensing Board
(919) 715-0991; fax 1378
410 N. Boylan Avenue, Raleigh, NC 27603

Board of Landscape Architects
(919) 850-9088
PO Box 41225, Raleigh, NC 27629

Landscape Contractors Registration Board: (919) 266-8070
P.O. Box 1578, Knightdale, NC 27545

Board of Law Examiners
(919) 828-4886
PO Box 2946, Raleigh, NC 27602

Public Librarian Certification Commission
(919) 733-2570
109 E. Jones Street, Raleigh, NC 27601-2807

NC Locksmith Licensing Board
(919) 838-8782; fax (919) 833-5743
P.O. Box 10972, Raleigh, NC 27605

Board of Marriage and Family Therapy
(336) 794-3891
3000 Bethesda Place, Ste. 503, Winston-Salem, NC 27103

Board of Massage and Bodywork Therapy
(919) 546-0050
PO Box 2539, Raleigh, NC 27602

NC Medical Board
800-253-9653
1201 Front St., Suite 100, Raleigh, NC 27609

Midwifery Joint Committee
(919) 782-3211
PO Box 2129, Raleigh, NC 27602

Board of Mortuary Science
(919) 733-9380; 800-862-0636
PO Box 27368, Raleigh, NC 27611-7368

Board of Nursing
(919) 782-3211; fax 781-9461
PO Box 2129, Raleigh, NC 27602

Board of Examiners of Nursing Home Administrators
(919) 571-4164
3733 National Dr., Suite 228, Raleigh, NC 27612

Board of Occupational Therapy
(919) 832-1380
PO Box 2280, Raleigh, NC 27602

Board of Opticians
(919) 733-9321
PO Box 25336, Raleigh, NC 27611-5336

Board of Examiners in Optometry
910-285-3160; 800-426-4457
109 N. Graham Street, Wallace, NC 28466-0609

Board of Practicing Pastoral Counselors
336-794-3470
1001 S Marshall St., Suite 5,
Winston-Salem, NC 27101-5893

Board of Pharmacy
(919) 942-4454
PO Box 459, Carrboro, NC
27510-0459

Board of Physical Therapy Examiners
(919) 490-6393; 800-800-8982
18 West Colony Plaza, Suite 140,
Durham, NC 27705

Board of Plumbing, Heating, and Fire
Sprinkler Contractors
(919) 875-3612; fax 3616
3801 Wake Forest Road, Suite 201,
Raleigh, NC 27609

Board of Podiatry Examiners
(919) 787-5181
1500 Sunday Drive, Ste. 102, Raleigh,
NC 27607

Private Protective Services
(919) 875-3611
1631 Midtown Place, Ste. 104,
Raleigh, NC 27609

Psychology Board
828-262-2258
895 State Farm Rd., Suite 101,
Boone, NC 28607

Real Estate Commission
(919) 875-3700
PO Box 17100, Raleigh, NC
27619-7100

Board of Refrigeration Examiners
(919) 755-5022
PO Box 10666, Raleigh, NC 27605

North Carolina Respiratory Care Board
(919) 878-5595; fax (919) 878-5565
1100 Navaho Drive, Suite 242,
Raleigh, North Carolina 27609

Board of Sanitarian Examiners
(919) 212-2006
5025 Harbor Towne Dr., Raleigh,
NC 27604

Certification Board for Social Work
336-625-1679
PO Box 1043, Asheboro, NC 27204

Board for Licensing Soil Scientists
(919) 515-2643
PO Box 5316, Raleigh,
NC 27650-5316

Board of Speech and Language
Pathologists and Audiologists
336-272-1828
PO Box 16885, Greensboro, NC
27416-0885

Substance Abuse Professionals
Certification Board
(919) 832-0975; fax 833-5743
800-248-2466 (Training Line)
PO Box 10126, Raleigh, NC 27605

Therapeutic Recreation Certification
Board
336-376-0050
PO Box 67, Saxapahaw, NC 27340

Board of Veterinary Medicine
(919) 733-7689
PO Box 12587, Raleigh, NC 27605

Index

Abandoned Property 86, 87
Abortion Data Collected by Department of Human Resources 41
Absentee Ballot Registers 154
Accident/incident Investigation Reports 59
Acquiring Control of Insurers 54
Adjudicatory Hearings for Juveniles 36
Administration of Abandoned Property 86
Administrative Hearings 38, 85, 123
Administrative Office of the Courts 34, 38, 42, 71, 72
Adoption
    Adoptions 84
    Orders 154
    Records 48, 146
Advance Publications, Inc. v. Elizabeth City 6, 10, 141
Agents 27, 40, 46, 51, 52, 56, 63
Agriculture
    Statistics 77
    Department of 154
Aid to the Needy Blind 81
Air Pollution Reports 116
Alamance County 136
Albemarle 138
Alcoholic Beverage Election Petitions 44
Allegheny County 136
Amusement Device Safety Act 71, 72
Animal Research 145
Annexation 128, 132
    Municipal, Maps and Ordinances 155, 156
Annual Reports 52, 69, 85, 121, 125, 127, 129, 156, 157
    on Bank Takeovers 48
Appointments to State Boards, Commissions, Etc. 156
Arbitral Tribunals 34
Areas of Environmental Concern 82
Arrest Records 37, 150
Arson 52
Articles of Organization 157
Ashe County 136
Assessment on Hog Purchases 79
Assumed Business Names 154, 155
Athlete Agents 63

Attorney
    General's Office 59, 91, 112
    Licensing Records 64
    Fees 16, 17, 30, 31, 144-146
    -client Communications 105, 144
Audiologists 70, 150
Audit Work Papers 122
Autopsies 100
Averasboro 138
Avery County 136
Bail Bondsmen and Runners 58
Bald Head Island 138
Ballot Counting 131
Banking (Banks) 7, 9, 48, 49, 51, 108, 127, 150
    Examiners 49
Bankruptcy Records 155
Banner Elk 138
Beaufort County 27, 143
Beech Mountain 138
Bid Analysis and Management System 113
Bidding, State and Local Gov't. Contracts 112, 113-115
    for State Government Supplies 114
Birth Certificates 98, 155, 157
Blowing Rock 138
Board Investigations of Engineers and Surveyors 65
Board of
    Awards 117
    Cosmetic Art Examiners 65
    Examiners for Speech and Language Pathologists 70, 150
    Podiatry Examiners 68
    Transportation 121
    Community Colleges 119
    County Commissioners 20, 77, 123
    Education 84, 85, 107, 119
Bond Issues 89
Boone 138
Broadcasting 23, 119
Budgets 7, 9, 127, 150
Building Code Council 115
Burke County 136
Bus Company Rates 60
Business
    Corporations 52, 156
    Inventories (for tax purposes) 76
    Licenses 156
    Projects (and Industrial) 111, 112

Businesses	4, 27, 57, 60, 76, 78, 87, 107, 111
Cabarrus County	136
Cancer Registry	99
Cardiac Rehabilitation Programs	103
Carteret County	136
Cary	138
Caswell Beach	138
Caucuses	118
Censure or Removal of Judges	35
Census of Children with Special Needs	84
Central Registry of Child Abuse	35
Certain Public Hospital Equipment	114
Certificates of Disability	45
Certification of Holdings	87
Change in Control of Banks	49
Chatham County	137
Child Abuse	39, 91, 111
Abuse and Neglect Cases	36
Abuse, Neglect and Dependency Cases	35
Child	
Custody and Visitation Mediation	48
Day-care Commission	80
Support - Location of Absent Parents	80
Children with Special Needs	84, 85
Chiropractors	67, 102, 151
Chowan County	137
Cities and Towns (also see Municipalities and Townships)	2, 135
Annexation	128
Boundaries	123
Council Minutes	129
Councils	124-126
Maps and Ordinances	155, 156
Service Districts	126
Civil Actions	16, 29, 34, 40, 119, 154
Claims Against Local Government Officials	129
Classification of Children with Special Needs	85
Clerks of Court	13, 133, 148
Clerks of Superior Court - Court Records	34
Cleveland County	137
Client Information	90, 91, 121, 149
Closed Sessions	1, 18, 24-26, 28, 106, 119, 120, 144
Coastal	
Fisheries - Referenda for Assessments	81
Land-use Plans	82
Resources Commission	82
Collision Reports	37, 46, 152, 155

Columbus	138
Commercial Fertilizer Grade-tonnage Reports	78
Commission for the Blind	120

Commissioner of
- Banks 48, 49
- Insurance 52-58, 86

Commissions	9, 19, 32, 118, 119, 127, 129, 130, 156
Committees	19, 32, 62, 81, 90, 101, 103, 104, 114, 118, 119
Committees and Standing Subcommittees	32, 118
Commodities Trading	63
Communicable Diseases	99

Communications Between
- Clergy and Communicants 39
- Physician and Patient 38
- Psychologist and Client 39

Community
- Advisory Committees 101, 104
- College Records and Meetings 86, 119
- Information on Hazardous Chemicals 73, 74

Company Documents	157
Competitive Health Care Information	102

Complaint
- Investigations 103
- State/regional Agencies, Boards 121

Comprehensive Major Medical Plan	113
Condemnation Proceedings	17
Conditional Sales Contracts	155
Condominium Declarations	155
Conference Committees	118

Confidential of
- Business Information 78, 116
- File of Motor Vehicle Registrations 46
- Information 12, 13, 15, 26, 34, 38, 44, 49-51, 75, 76, 81, 84, 87, 89, 91, 94 95, 97, 99, 101, 119, 120, 126, 151
- Juvenile Records 37
- Tax Information 106

Conover	138
Conservation Agreements	155
Construction and Repair Work	115
Construction Diaries and Bid Analyses	113

Contested Case
    Administrative Hearings 123
    Hearings 44
Continuing Care Facilities 58
Contractors 28, 64, 65, 112, 148
Contracts 57, 59, 60, 83, 101, 102, 112-115, 127, 128, 150, 155, 156
    Negotiations 27
    Services and Equipment 114
Controlled Substance
    Records 71
    Tax 76
    Substances 70-72, 76
Copying 11-13, 16, 17, 24, 34, 49, 63, 66, 76, 79, 88, 89, 128, 132
Corporate Merger or Consolidation Certificates 155
Corporations 10, 19, 52, 60, 101, 114, 141, 155-157
Cosmetologist Records 65
Counselor Privilege 39, 40, 44
Counselors 37, 39, 68, 149
County and Municipal (also see Cities and Towns)
    Managers' Annual Reports 125
    Ordinance Books 125
    Tax Assessors 76
    Service Districts 126
Courts 3, 16, 17, 30, 33-36, 42, 71, 72, 105, 110
    Minutes 154
    Records 34, 38, 91
    Shall Be Open 33, 118
Credentialing and Peer Review Information at Public Hospitals 102
Credit Union Division Records 50
Crime Victim
    Compensation
        Commission 44
        Reports 43
    Victim Information 43
Criminal
    Actions 34, 154
    Cases 42, 43, 111
    Intelligence Information 109
    Investigations 28, 109, 111
    Record Checks of
        Employees of Hospitals 83
        School Employees 82
Crop Sales Contracts 155
Cumberland County 136
Currituck County 137
Customer Information Submitted to 911 60

Dam Safety Law	116
Dare County	137
Davidson County	137
Davie County	137
Day Care Inspection Plans	80
Death Certificates	155, 157
Debt Collection	77
Decisions of Commissioner of Banks	49
Decrees of Title to Land	155
Deeds of Trust	49, 155
DEHNR	156
Deliberative Process Privilege	7, 134
Delinquency Records	36
Delinquent and Undisciplined Juveniles	37
Dentist Licensing and Disciplinary Records	67

Department of
    Correction 41, 121, 123, 141, 142
    Correction Rules 121
    Department of Corrections 41, 91, 102, 123
    Labor 53, 56, 61, 71, 100
        Investigation Records 71
    Public Instruction 84, 85, 100
    Transportation 113, 114

Depository for Wills	47
Developmental Disabilities	83, 89, 90
Deviations from Established Rates	56
Diaries	113
Disabilities	83, 89, 90, 121, 149, 150, 152
Disclosure of Confidential Information by Legislators	87
Discovery	42, 71, 76, 86, 102, 111, 116, 141, 145
Civil Actions - Protective Orders	34
Criminal Cases - Protective Orders	43
Discrimination Investigations and Proceedings	135

Disposition
    Records 111, 149
    Hearings for Juveniles 36

Division of
    Criminal Information 82
    Motor Vehicles 13, 16, 37, 45, 46, 81, 152
    Veteran Affairs 132, 133, 148
    Youth Services 36, 37, 112

DNA Database	42
Doctors	41, 99, 146
Domiciliary Homes	100-103
Drainage Assessments	154
Drainage District	19, 145

Drivers License
    Administration 45
    Denial Proceedings 45
    Records 16, 155
Drug Addiction 45
Duplin County 137
Durham 6, 96, 135, 136, 141, 142
Durham County 135
Durham Herald Co. v. North Carolina Low-level Radioactive Waste 6, 142
Durham Herald Co., Inc. v. County of Durham 141
Easement Deeds 155
Economic Development Board 121
Edgecombe County 135
Education 31, 70, 83-85, 97, 107, 119, 135, 142, 152
Eggimann v. Wake County Board of Education 142
Election
    Precinct Maps 131, 155
    Results 154-156
Elections 44, 88, 124, 130-132, 148, 154
    Board of Dental Examiners 67
    County Boards of 154
Electric Membership Corporations, Mergers and Consolidations 155, 156
Electronic Meetings 22, 119
Elementary and Secondary Education 83
Elevator Safety Act 71, 72
Elizabeth City 6, 10, 138, 141
Emergency
    Meetings 21, 22, 24, 124
    Telephone Systems 60
Eminent Domain - Memorandum of Action by Landowner 155
Employment Discrimination Complaints 38
Employment Security Commission 74
Energy Division of Department of Commerce 122
Energy
    Information Reporting System 82
    Policy Council 82
Environmental Management Commission 116, 119, 121
    Investigation 115
Escheated and Abandoned Property 86
Evaluations in Incompetency Proceedings 47
Exceptions to Public Records Law Disclosure 133
Executors and Administrators of Estates, Appointment 154
Experience Rate Modifier 56
Expunction of
    Criminal Charges 42
    Juvenile Criminal Convictions 38

Records	37, 38, 42, 70
Extension of Water and Sewer Districts	130
Facilities for People with Mental Illnesses	89
Family Therapist	39
Farmworker Health Hazards	100
Fayetteville	3, 136

Federal
- Electoral Candidate Information Reports 132
- Government Agencies 1, 9

Fee-based Practicing Pastoral Counselors	68
Financial Privacy Act	50, 153
Financing Statements for Secured Transactions	47

Fire
- Chiefs 73
- Investigation Reports 59
- Sprinkler Contractors 64, 65, 148

Fisheries	81
Food and Beverage Tax Returns	136
Food, Drug and Cosmetic Act	77
Foreclosures	155
Forest Product Assessments	82
Franklin County	135
Franklinton	135
Fraud Records	52
Freedom of Information Act	1, 9
Fuel Prices	62
Gag Orders	35
Garner	138
Gaston County	137
Gastonia	136
General Contractors	64
Genetic Engineering Review Board	78
Genetically Engineered Organisms	78
Geographical Information Systems	112
Geologist Licensing Records	65
Gift Deeds	155

Government
- Contracting Procedures 114
- Contracts 115
- Election Funds 132

Governor's Advocacy Council for Persons with Disabilities	121
Grand Jury Proceedings	42
Grantor and Grantee Indexes	155
Granville County	137
Greensboro	135, 136
Guardians	36, 84, 154

Guardians Ad Litem 36
Halifax County 137
Hazardous Chemical Emergency Information 73
Hazardous Substance 115, 116
    Trade Secret Information 73
Health
    Assessments 100
    -care Liability Insurance Records 86
    Departments 93, 94, 98, 148
    Maintenance Organizations 58
Henderson County 137
Hertford County 137
Hickory 138
High Point City Council 23, 125, 143
High Rock Lake Marine Commission 62
Highway Construction Bids 113
Hillsborough 136
Holden Beach 138
Holding Companies 54
Home Care Agencies 102, 103
Honorary Degrees, Scholarships, Prizes and Awards 26
Hospital
    Cooperative Agreements 104
    Inspections 101
    Medical Review Committees 101
    Patient Information Provided to the 102
Housing Authority 17, 127, 142
Husband and Wife 36, 44
    as Witness in Civil Actions 40
    as Witness in Criminal Action 40
In re Hayes 92, 142
In re Norwell 34, 143
In re Southern Bell Tel. & Tel. Co. 43, 142
Incapacity of Criminal Defendants to Proceed with Trial 43
Incompetence 45
Incompetency Proceedings 47
Incorporations 132, 155
Index of Regular License Plates on Highway Patrol Vehicles 46
Industries 27

Information
    Obtained by Guardians Ad Litem in 36
    on Archaeological Resources 61
    on Petroleum Supplies 122
Inmate Grievances 123
Inspection
    of Archived Public Records 89
    Departments 155
    of Nursing Homes 102
Inspections 10, 57, 78, 80, 101, 102, 126, 155
Insurance
    Information and Privacy Act 56
    Acquiring Control of Insurers 54
    Annual Actuary Reports for Life Insurance 57
    Application for License as Third Party 57
    Attorney General Fire Investigation Reports 59
    Bail Bondsmen and Runners 58
    Books and Records of Third Party 57
    Commissioner Proceedings 55
    Commissioner Records 52
    Deviations from Established Rates 56
    Experience Rate Modifier Information 56
    Filings of North Carolina Rate Bureau 55
    Health Maintenance Organizations 58
    Insurance Holding Companies 54
    Investigations of Continuing Care Facilities 58
    License Revocations 53
    Life and Health Insurance 57
    North Carolina Health Care Excess 56
    Patient Medical Records 53
    Payroll Deduction Insurance Proposals 55
    Postassessment Insurance Guaranty 56
    Public Officers and Employees Liability 55
Rate Filings 56
Rate Lists 52
Records and Proceedings of Insurers 54
Records of Examinations 53
Records of Negotiations and Meetings 58
Regulatory Information System Information 53
State Fire and Rescue Commission 58
Investigation Records 16, 18, 71, 109, 111, 115, 120, 134, 135
    of Child Abuse, Neglect or Dependency 35
Investment Advisors 63
Jacksonville Daily News Co. V. Onslow County Bd. Of Educ 18, 31, 83, 143
Jail Inspections 126
Joint

    Legislative Commission on Governmental Operations 114
    Meetings of Legislative Budget Committees 114
    Municipal Electric Agencies 127
Judgments 34, 129, 154, 157
Judicial
    Review of Admissions to Facilities 92
    Reviews Related to Administrative 55
    Standards Commission 35, 117
Juries 117
    Lists 40, 41
Juvenile
    Actions 34, 154
    Delinquency Records 36
    Proceedings 44, 118
    Records 37, 44, 151
Kindergarten Children in Public Schools 100
Kinston 138
Lake Wylie Marine Commission 62
Land
    Conveyances 156
    Grant Judgments 157
    Grants from the State of North Carolina, Plats, Surveys 157
    Plats 47
Landscape Contractor Register 65
Law Examiners 64
Lease or Sale of Public Hospitals to Corporations 101
Leases of Real Estate 156
Lee County 137
Legislative 18, 19, 81, 114, 122, 124, 131
    Access to State Agency Information 87
    Commissions 32, 118
    Committee on New Licensing Boards 89
    Ethics Committee 88, 117, 118
    Proposals 119
Legislators and Legislative Employees, Conversations between 88
Legitimization of Children, Orders for 154
Lenoir County 137
Library User Records 93
License
    Boards 3, 61, 69, 89, 117
    Dentists 67
    Podiatrists 68
    Records 64, 65
    Revocations 53
Licensure 70, 96, 150
Liens 34, 154

Life and Health Insurance Guaranty Association 57, 58
Limited
    Liability Companies 52, 157
    Partnerships 157
Lincoln County 137
Lis Pendens 34, 154
Lists... .... 2, 3, 38, 40-42, 51, 52, 79, 84, 88, 98, 107, 115, 130, 131, 135, 149
    of Escheated and Abandoned Property 86
    of Partners in Professional Partnerships 60
Lobbyist Expense Reports 87
Local
    Boards 84-86, 107
    Employees 38, 107, 115
    Government Bond Orders 127
    Government Budgets 127
    Government Small Contracts 115
    Governmental Employees' Retirement System 98
    Preservation Commission Meetings 129
    Tax Records 107
Local Water Safety Committee Meetings 62
Long-term Care Ombudsmen 121
Macon 21, 124, 146
Mailing 14, 76, 79
Managers' Annual Reports 125
Marine Fisheries Commission 81
Marital Counseling Information 39
Marriage
    Certificates 156
    Licenses 156
    Settlements 156
Martin County 137
Media 12, 14, 21-23, 57, 96, 97, 112, 131, 132, 150, 151
Medical
    Plan 113
    Records 38, 53, 100-103
    in Possession of Department of Health 120
    in the Public Health System 98
    Subpoenaed in Civil Actions 34
    Review Committees 101
Meetings
    and Annual Reports of Regional Councils of Government 129
    of North Carolina Medical Veterinary Board 68
    of Regional Sports Authorities 129
Mental
    Health Area Authorities 93
    Health Authorities 83

Health Contract Agencies	83
Illnesses	89, 90
Metropolitan Water District Financial Reports	130

Military
Discharges	156
Surplus Registers	98

Mine
Accident Reports	61
Safety Advisory Council	61

Minutes	7, 9, 16, 24, 25, 27, 30, 34, 55, 106, 118-121 127, 129, 134, 144150, 154
Local Boards of Education	85
of Proceedings	124
Mitchell County	137
Mooresville	138
Mortgages	49, 156

Motor
Collision Reports	46, 155
Contract Carrier Rates	60
Division of	155
Fuel Prices	62
Registration	82, 155
Vehicle	45, 46, 82, 155, 157

Municipalities and Townships	138
Annexation	128
Boundaries	123
Councils	124-126
Maps and Ordinances	155, 156
Service Districts	126
Mutual Burial Association Commission	122
Name Changes	154
Nash County	137
National Guard Records	97
Natural Gas Pipeline Accident Reports	59
Neglect Cases	36
New Hanover County	136
News & Observer Pub. Co. v. Poole	7, 24, 26, 96, 105, 106, 118, 133, 134, 143
News & Observer Pub. Co. v. Wake County Hospital System, Inc.	6, 144
Nonprofit Corporations	52, 157

North Carolina
Appraisal Board	70
Board for the Licensing of	65
Board of Opticians	68
Center for Missing Persons	122
Child Fatality Prevention System	119
Controlled Substances Act	70, 71

  Government Agencies 14
  Health Care Excess Liability Fund 56
  Hearing Aid Dealers and Fitters Board 70
  Housing Finance Agency 89
  Housing Finance Agency Bond Issues 89
  Industrial Commission 75
  Landscape Contractors' Licensing Board 65
  Medical Database Commission 104
  Partnership for Children, Inc. 120
  Radiation Protection Act 75
  Rate Bureau 55, 56
  Real Estate Commission 69
  State Bar 64
  State Board of Examiners of 68
  State University 84
North Carolina Press Asso. v Spangler 7, 10, 17, 144
Not Subject to the Open Meetings Law 24, 25, 32, 117, 118, 120, 134, 144
Notice of Official Meetings 20, 24
Nursing
  Home 83, 102
      Advisory Committees 104
      Complaint Investigations 103
      Patient Bill of Rights 103
  Pools and Hospices 103
Oaths of Public Officials 157
Occupational Licensing
  Board Annual Reports 69, 157
  Boards 69, 117
Occupational Safety and Health
  Act 72, 74
  Records 72
  Programs of State and Local 72
Official Meetings of Public Bodies 4, 16, 19-26, 86, 118, 124
Official Records of Commissioner of Banks 49
Officials of the State 119
Officials Whose Safety Is at Risk 46
Oil Pollution and Hazardous Substances Control Act 115, 116
Opticians 68
Options to Purchase Land 156
Optometrists 38, 146
Orange County 136
Ordinances 2, 125, 127, 135, 155-157
Organizations Receiving State Funds 114
Outcome-based Education Program 85
Oyster Grants 157
Parole Commission 41, 142

Partitions of Land 156
Partnerships 60, 61, 120, 157
    Certificates 156
Pasquotank County 137
Pastoral Counselors 68
Patient Information 103
    at Health Care Facilities 102
    Obtained in Dentist Peer Reviews 67
    Obtained in Physician 67
Patient Medical Records 53, 98, 103, 120
Pay Raises 18, 31, 83, 143
Peer Review Committees 90, 101, 103
Peer Reviews of Impaired Physicians 67
Pender County 137
Permitted Purposes for Holding 26
Personnel Records of Government Employees 2, 33, 93
Petroleum
    Leases 156
    Supplies 122
Pharmacy Records 70
Physician 34, 36, 102, 146
    Assistant Peer Reviews 67
    Licensing and Disciplinary Records 66
    Privileges 66
    Privileges and Malpractice Insurance 66
    Physician-patient Privilege 38, 39, 44, 146
    Privilege Waived in Child Abuse Cases 39
Piedmont Publishing Co. v. City of Winston-Salem 42, 145
Pitt County 137
Plats   47, 61, 156, 157
Postassessment Insurance Guaranty Association 56
Poultry Products Inspection Act Information 78
Powers of Attorney 156
Precious Metals Dealers 61
Preliminary Drafts 7
Presentence Reports 43
Pre-adoption Reports 47
Prisoners 41, 123, 142
Privacy 4, 4, 7, 43, 50, 56, 85, 133, 142, 145, 153
Private Personnel Service Advisory Council 71
Probable Cause Hearings for Juveniles 14 and Older 36
Probation Officers' Records; Parole Records 41
Proceedings of State Board of Education 83
Professional
    Corporations 157
    Liability Insurance Annual Statements 53

Property
    Records 86
    Tax Appraisal.. 77
Proposed
    Changes for Bus Company Rates 60
    Changes in Public Utility Rates... 59
    Property Tax Appraisal Schedules 77
Prosecution for Revealing Confidential Information 49
Protective Orders 34, 43
Psychologist Licensing and Disciplinary Records 68
Psychology Board 68
Public
    Assistance Recipients 80, 151
    Bodies 1, 4, 18-26, 28, 106, 116-118, 124
    Burning 52
    Comment 123
    Contract Bidding 112
    Hearings 4, 22, 125, 126, 130
    Hospital Boards 32, 116
    Housing Authority Hearings 127
    Land 114
    Law Enforcement Agencies 109
    Officers and Employees Liability Insurance Commission 55
    Policy 5, 7, 18, 30, 133, 134, 145
        Exceptions to Public Records Law.. 133
    Records Defined 5
    School
        Student Records 85
        Teacher Complaint/commendation Files.................................. 85
Publishers 84
Quarterly Financial Reports.. 122
Radiation Protection Act... 75
Radioactive Waste Management Commission 76
Rape Victims 40
Rate
    Bureau 55, 56
    Filings 56
    Lists 52

Real Property
    Estate Appraisers 70
    Conveyances to the State 157
Receipt of Public Assistance 79
Record of Registered Barbers and Apprentices 64
Recording 23, 85, 119
Records of
    Plumbing, Heating, and Fire Sprinkler 64
    Property Deposited to Escheat Fund 86
    Treatment for Drug Dependence 71
    Relating to Children with Special Needs 84
    Relating to Drivers Licenses 45
Redevelopment Commissions 129, 130
Regional
    Planning Commissions 127
    Solid Waste Management Authorities 127
    Sports Authorities 129
Register of Deeds 3, 40, 47, 98, 155
Registered Public Obligations 128
Registers of Absentee Ballots 131
Registrations 46
Registry of
    Licensed Electrical Contractors 65
    Textbook Publisher Representatives 84
Regular and Special Meetings of City and Town Councils 128
Regular Meetings 20, 21, 122, 123, 128
Regulatory Information System Information 53
Removal of District Attorneys 34
Renunciation of
    Property Succession Rights 154
    Real Property Rights 156
Repayment of Money Owed by Employees 119
Reports of
    Leaf Tobacco Sold 78
    State Officers 157
    Board of Medical Examiners 66
Requests for Examinations of Delinquent Insurers 58
Responses to Inmate Grievances 123
Retaliatory Employment Actions 74
Revenue Statistics 76
Review Hearings for Juvenile Placements 36
Revocation of Drivers License 45
Room Occupancy and Tourism Development Tax Returns 136

Rosters of 64-66, 69, 70
    Licensed Contractors 64
Rowan County 137
Rules of Commission of Youth Services 112
Runaways 37
Rutherford County 137
Safety and Health Review Board 72
Sales 155, 156
Savings Bank and Savings and Loan Association 51
Savings Institutions Division 51
School Counselor Privilege 39, 44
Scrap Purchasers 60
Search Warrants 80, 111, 152, 154
Secretary of State 20, 62-64, 69, 87, 156
    Interrogatories to Corporations 52
    Office of 47
Securities Dealers and Salesmen Registration 62
Service
    Contracts 59, 60
    Districts 126
    Regulations 59, 60
Sessions 1, 18, 24-26, 28, 89, 106, 119, 120, 144
Settlement
    Records 108
    Housing Discrimination Cases 47
Sewage Pretreatment Program Applications 115
Social Security Numbers 45, 98, 104, 107, 113, 152
    Automobile Registration 46
Social Services Commission 35
Social Worker Privilege 40, 44
Solid Waste Management 99, 127
Southeast Interstate Low-level Radioactive 76
Southport 139
Special Assessments by Counties and Municipalities 126
Speech and Language Pathologists and Audiologists 70, 150
State
    Advisory Council on Occupational Safety and Health 72
    Auditor 114, 122
    Auditor Investigations 122
    Auditor Work Papers 122
    Banking Commission 48
    Board of Education 83, 84
    Board of Elections 130-132
    Board of Examiners of Electrical Contractors 65
    Board of Examiners of Plumbing 65, 148
    Board of Sanitarian Examiners 69

    Bureau of Investigation 42, 59, 96, 134
    Center for Health Statistics 100
    Employees 55, 78, 82, 93, 95-97, 106, 107, 152
    Government 20, 108, 114, 117
    Health Plan Purchasing Alliance Board 120
    Health Plan Purchasing Alliances 120
    Libraries and Publications 93
    Licensing Board for General Contractors 64
    or Local Employees 115
    Treasurer 86, 89, 122
        Quarterly Financial Reports 122
Statewide Student Testing Program Scores 85
Statistics 55, 71, 76, 77, 84, 98, 100, 157
Student Records 85
Subdivisions 5, 8, 9, 15, 18, 19, 72, 156
Substance Abuse 83, 92, 93
    Problems 89, 90
Sunset Beach 139
Superintendent of Public Instruction 83, 84
Supply Purchases 114
Surveyors 65
Suspension, Removal, and Reinstatement of Magistrates 35
Tarboro 135
Tax 7, 9, 18, 75-77, 87, 95, 97, 106, 127, 135, 136, 150, 152
    Listing Abstracts 6, 76, 107, 148
Taxpayer
    Information Held by State Agencies 77
    Bill of Rights 76
Teacher
    Complaint/commendation Files 85
    Contracts 83, 150
Teachers' and State Employees'
    Comprehensive Major Medical Plan 113
    Retirement System 113
Technical Ordinances 125
Tender Offer Disclosures 63
Tender Offers 63
Termination of Parental Rights 36
Test Drilling or Boring 113, 114
    on Public Land 114
Textbook Lists 84, 149
Third Party Administrators 57
Timber Sales Contracts 156
Time Shares 156
Title Transfers (Land Titles) 156
Towns and Township (see Municipalities and Townships; Cities and Towns)

Toxic Vapors Act - Conditional Discharge 72
Trade Secrets 18, 26, 34, 50, 57, 72, 75, 78, 107, 108, 114, 115, 143
Trademark Registration 64
Trailer Park Permit 31
Transfers of Prisoners to Other States 123
Treatment for Drug Dependence 71
Unclaimed and Abandoned Property 87
Underground Utilities 155, 156
Uniform Education Reporting System 84
University of North Carolina 4, 19, 86
Uranium Exploration Information 61
Urban Service Districts 126
Utilities
    Accounts 7, 9, 127, 150
    Commission 59, 60
    Accident/incident 59
    Hearings 59
    Records of Activities 59
    Rates, Service Regulations, and Service 59
    Underground, ... 155, 156
Vance County 138
Veteran Affairs 132, 133, 148
Vital Statistics, State Registrar of 157
Vocational Rehabilitation Advisory Council Annual Report 119
Voter Registration 130, 155
    for Municipal Annexations 132
    Records 130, 155
Wage and Hour Act 71
Wake County
    Board of Education 31, 142
    Hospital System, Inc. 6, 9, 144
Wake Forest 139
Washington 138, 139
Washington County 138
Water and Air Pollution Reports 116
Water
    Capacity Use Areas 115
    Resources Records 119
    Safety Committee Meetings 62
Watercraft Registration Records 62
Wetlands 156
Wildlife Resources Commission 62
Wilkes General Hospital 116
Wills 47, 154, 157
Workers' Compensation 53, 56, 74
Yancey County 138

Yaupon Beach... 139